CITYSPOTS
PISA

Tracey Johnson

KT-377-045

Written by Tracey Johnson

Published by Thomas Cook Publishing
A division of Thomas Cook Tour Operations Limited
Company registration No: 3772199 England
The Thomas Cook Business Park, 9 Coningsby Road
Peterborough PE3 8SB, United Kingdom
Email: books@thomascook.com, Tel: +44 (0)1733 416477
www.thomascookpublishing.com

Produced by The Content Works Ltd
Aston Court, Kingsmead Business Park, Frederick Place
High Wycombe, Bucks HP11 1LA
www.thecontentworks.com

Series design based on an original concept by Studio 183 Limited

ISBN: 978-1-84848-081-0

First edition © 2009 Thomas Cook Publishing
Text © Thomas Cook Publishing
Maps © Thomas Cook Publishing/PCGraphics (UK) Limited
Transport map © Communicarta Limited

Series Editor: Lucy Armstrong
Production/DTP: Steven Collins

Printed and bound in Spain by GraphyCems

Cover photography (Torre Pendente and Fontana dei Putti) © Picture Partners/Alamy

CITYSPOTS
PISA

Thomas Cook

WHAT'S IN YOUR GUIDEBOOK?

Independent authors Impartial up-to-date information from our travel experts who meticulously source local knowledge.

Experience Thomas Cook's 165 years in the travel industry and guidebook publishing enriches every word with expertise you can trust.

Travel know-how Thomas Cook has thousands of staff working around the globe, all living and breathing travel.

Editors Travel-publishing professionals, pulling everything together to craft a perfect blend of words, pictures, maps and design.

You, the traveller We deliver a practical, no-nonsense approach to information, geared to how you really use it.

ABOUT THE AUTHOR

Tracey Johnson was born in Yorkshire and emigrated to Italy in 1992. A freelance journalist and a teacher of English as a foreign language, Tracey, who is in thrall to all things Tuscan (and Pisan in particular), has been published in the specialist press all over the world.

CONTENTS

SYMBOLS KEY

The following symbols are used throughout this book:

ⓐ address ☏ telephone ⓦ website address ⓔ email
🕒 opening times Ⓝ public transport connections ❶ important

The following symbols are used on the maps:

i information office   ▪ points of interest
✈ airport   O city
➕ hospital   O large town
🛡 police station   ○ small town
🚌 bus station   ═ motorway
🚆 railway station   — main road
✝ cathedral   — minor road
❶ numbers denote   — railway
  featured cafés & restaurants

Hotels and restaurants are graded by approximate price as follows:
£ budget price ££ mid-range price £££ expensive

▶ *Pisa Cathedral and the Leaning Tower, Campo dei Miracoli*

Introduction

Pisa's iconic building is, of course, its Torre Pendente, or Leaning Tower, which continues to defy gravity and stands – but not straight – in the aptly named Campo dei Miracoli (Field of Miracles). This beautiful square, dotted with white buildings and surrounded by green lawns, is the city's focal point and also contains a trio of symbolic sights: the Duomo (cathedral) stands for life; the Battistero (baptistery) represents its beginning; and Camposanto (cemetery) its end.

The majority of visitors to Pisa stay only for the day and tend to remain in and around the Campo dei Miracoli. This is a wasted opportunity as this West Tuscan city has a great deal more to offer. The city's rich culture is fed by its Etruscan and Roman past, which is evident as you walk around and discover the many beautiful buildings, especially the churches which are packed with the most glorious art. Indeed a characteristic of Pisa is the elegance with which the past and the present come together: the medieval streets, the tower houses, the exuberant student population, the magnificent architecture that dates back to the Romanesque period, the waterfront along the river Arno and the large immigrant community – all these and more combine to produce Pisa, a busy cosmopolitan city with a stunningly picturesque landscape.

This is an inspired and inspirational destination. As a renowned centre of learning that's famous for its universities and research laboratories, Pisa stands out even in the intellectually eminent context of Italian cities.

If you venture out through Pisa's many doorways along the

city walls you'll find nature reserves, interesting ancient ruins, delectably pretty villages and more. While the city is undoubtedly an ideal portal to the delights of Tuscany, one of Italy's most beautiful regions, Pisa is a place that merits serious investigation in its own right.

▲ *Take time to explore Pisa's medieval streets and alleyways*

When to go

SEASONS & CLIMATE

The best times to visit Pisa are spring or autumn. Summer's humidity invites airborne pests, and August in particular can be uncomfortably muggy. In the summer months temperatures range between 25–30°C (77–86°F); winter temperatures seldom drop below zero, remaining around 10–15°C (50–59°F). November tends to be the wettest month.

ANNUAL EVENTS

January

Forever Sposi Wedding-related exhibition at Stazione Leopolda.
ⓐ Piazza Guerrazzi ❶ (050) 215 31 Ⓦ www.foreversposi.it

February

Carnival in Viareggio Expect maximum fun as this town fills with carnival colour (see page 33). Ⓦ www.viareggio.ilcarnevale.com
Ⓝ Trains run regularly between Pisa Centrale and Viareggio

March

Expo Pisa The subject is broad: anything domestic is covered here. One could go in at a Cro-Magnon level of domestic prowess and emerge with a flair for interior design and strong opinions on garden feng shui. ⓐ Area Expo, Via Emilia, Ospedaletto
❶ (050) 777 176; during the Expo only (050) 985 567
Ⓦ www.expo-pisa.com

Capodanno Pisano In the Middle Ages New Year was celebrated on 25 March. Today Pisa marks that day with a special mass at the cathedral and a street parade. Call the tourist information office (see page 136) nearer the time for details.

April & May

Lus: Experiments Under the Tower Some very nifty demonstrations of science and technology aimed at children ⓐ Via Nicola Pisano 25 ⓣ (050) 315 3776 ⓛ Late Apr–late May ⓦ www.ludotecascientifica.it
Settimana delle Piagge Le Piagge park on Pisa's outskirts houses a flower market that turns into a fragrantly floral fiesta in honour of Sant'Ubaldo, who is, among other things, the patron saint of people with obsessive-compulsive disorder. ⓐ Viale delle Piagge

● *The famous Viareggio Carnival lasts for almost a month*

June

Gioco del Ponte On the last Sunday in June, locals dressed in medieval costume (play) fight on the bridges. The festival dates back to 1568, when the townsfolk pushed a carriage over the bridge. ⓐ Ponte di Mezzo

Regata delle Quattro Antiche Repubbliche Marinare A dramatic boat race between the historical maritime towns of Amalfi, Genoa, Venice and Pisa. Held in each of the participating towns on a rotating basis, it next takes place in Pisa in 2013.

Regata di San Ranieri Four rowing boat teams race in period costume in honour of the patron saint of Pisa (see page 14). ⏰ 17 June

August

Giornata di Festa nell'Anno Domini 1398 During the last week of the month, zealots from the world of historical reconstruction caper hither and thither in doublet and kirtle to recreate medieval social life in an Italian village. ⓐ Volterra ⓦ www.comune.volterra.pi.it ⓝ Trains run regularly from Pisa Centrale station to Volterra

September

Anima Mundi Classical music festival with concerts held daily all month in various locations. ⓣ (050) 560 547 ⓦ www.opapisa.it

Astiludio The first Sunday of the month sees people in costumes, this time from the 15th century, providing a glimpse of times gone by with a festival of games, flag-throwing and parades. ⓐ Piazza dei Priori, Volterra ⓦ www.sbandieratorivolterra.it

October

Palio del Papero (Duck Racing) Waddling and wobbling to the finish line, ducks compete against each other in this animal-friendly and charming event in the Pisan commune of San Miniato. A quacking time is guaranteed. ⓐ Balconevisi, San Miniato ⓣ (0571) 427 45 ⓦ www.cittadisanminiato.it ⓝ Bus: CPT bus services run regularly from Pisa to Pontedera and San Miniato

December

Pisa Vini Wine festival that attracts viticulturalists from all over Tuscany, held in the first week of the month. ⓐ Stazione Leopolda, Piazza Guerrazzi ⓣ (050) 215 31 ⓦ www.pisaunicaterradivino.it

PUBLIC HOLIDAYS
Capodanno (New Year's Day) 1 Jan
La Befana (Epiphany) 6 Jan
Pasqua & Lunedì di Pasqua (Easter Sunday & Monday)
4 & 5 Apr 2010; 24 & 25 Apr 2011
Festa della Liberazione (Liberation Day) 25 Apr
Festa del Lavoro (Labour Day) 1 May
Festa della Repubblica (Anniversary of the Republic) 2 June
Ferragosto (Feast of the Assumption) 15 Aug
Tutti Santi (All Saints' Day) 1 Nov
**Festa dell'Immacolata (Feast of the Immaculate
Conception)** 8 Dec
Natale (Christmas) 25 Dec
Santo Stefano (Boxing Day) 26 Dec

Luminara & Regata di San Ranieri

Of the multitude of wondrous sights on offer in Tuscany, quite the loveliest is that conjured each year on the evening of 16 June, when Pisa is lit by candles placed all along the river Arno. These Luminara, or illuminations of Saint Ranieri, patron saint of Pisa, send their light through thousands of smooth white glasses to create a shimmer that washes over the primarily white buildings of the city. At the same time, the Leaning Tower (see page 67) is lit from top to bottom with oil lamps, which are also placed all along the city wall, making the Campo dei Miracoli truly live up to its name.

On the day following this ineffably exquisite light show, the people of Pisa traditionally celebrate their patron saint, Ranieri, with a regatta. Four rowing teams representing Pisa's districts of St Martino, St Antonio, St Maria and St Francesco conform to the

local predilection for dressing in medieval costume and hurtle along the river Arno, whose banks throng with cheering locals. The winning team is the one whose climber manages to board a boat that counts as the finishing line and climb to the top of its high mast, bringing down the victory banner. The other teams are also awarded banners, while the last placed have to comfort themselves with a rather surreal consolation prize – geese.

This is a serious race, and the jostling as the four steersmen attempt to dominate the side of the Arno where the current is the most favourable frequently teeters on the edge of river rage. Once the race is over, the waterfront is packed with people walking along the river browsing at market stalls and waiting for the fireworks at midnight. Some take the opportunity to have dinner outside in candlelight. A special mass is held at the cathedral (see page 66), where the bones of St Ranieri are kept.

🔽 *Luminara brighten up the city with lights on the night of 16 June*

History

Although its origins are probably Etruscan, it was the Romans who made Pisa into a city, which they rather catchily named Colonia Julia Pisana Obsequens. The fact that the port was situated at the mouth of the river Arno made it an ideal naval base for the fleet of the Roman Empire, and, under Augustus's rule, the harbour, Via Aurelia and the city walls were built.

When the Empire disintegrated, Pisa's commercial and strategic importance ensured its prosperity. By the early Middle Ages, the city was a flourishing trading centre and influential cultural hub. Developing into a so-called Marine Republic, the city prosecuted naval battles against the Saracens, from which its fleet successfully returned home with enough booty to start building a cathedral.

Pisa's fall from its position of great influence came in the 14th century and was caused by the city's overstretching itself with continuous battles against the rival maritime cities of Genoa, Florence and Lucca. Following the assassination of its ruler Piero Gambacorti in 1392, Pisa's strength faltered, and for the next 500 years it came under Florentine rule, subsequently becoming part of Italy. In 1564, the city's most famous son, the astronomer and philosopher Galileo Galilei, was born and was subsequently educated at its university.

Accepting the sovereignty of the Florentine dynasty was not all bad for Pisa. The Medici government of Cosimo I brought something of a renaissance: universities were opened, government offices built and the Order of the Knights of St Stephen (see page 79) was instituted.

Pisa's reputation as a centre of academic excellence was cemented in the early 19th century, when the educational moderniser Gaetano Giorgini reformed its university and even went so far as to create the world's first seat of Agriculture and Sheep Farming. The city's progressive educational profile even stretched to the revolutionary student archetype: its university students took part in 1860's war of independence against Italy.

During the 20th-century era of fascism, Pisa's Athenaeum was a centre of political debate (and was decidedly anti-fascist).

World War II bombs destroyed much of the city and, in 1966, flooding led to the collapse of the Solferino Bridge and the destruction of Lungarno Pacinotti. Happily, 1967's opening of the Scuola Superiore Sant'Anna triggered a reversal of fortune and today Pisa is one of the richest university towns in the world.

● *Pisa is the birthplace of astronomer Galileo Galilei*

Lifestyle

Pisa, a city that attracts people who live unfussy lives that revolve around simple values. However, while Pisa and Pisans do strike the visitor as being refreshingly uncomplicated, it would be idle to pretend that the city is some sort of timeless Tuscan Dingley Dell. The promise – or should that be threat? – of tourism is looming large: new hotel complexes are being built in the coastal resort of Marina di Pisa, about 18 km (11 miles) to the west of the city centre; the beach is being cleaned and levelled out; and, a sure sign that the welcome mat is being unfurled with an eye to the tourist euro, today most Pisans speak some English.

Sundays tell you a lot about the lifestyle: the afternoon stroll hasn't gone out of fashion and it seems that everyone is out and about, happily eating ice cream and chatting.

Always friendly and willing to help, the Pisan people are proud of their city and its heritage. This civic pride leads many of them to take part in the re-enactment of the Gioco del Ponte incident and the San Ranieri celebrations in June (see pages 12 & 14). They are also fiercely proud of their Leaning Tower for its beauty and, it has to be said, celebrity status.

Pisa is a city whose inhabitants have always been open to outside influences. The great variety of architectural styles in monuments shows how much exposure to different people and other cultures the Pisans have had in the past, as they successfully adapted to a changing world. Thus the locals tend to be outward-looking, interested in others and inclusive.

The university campus fills the city with young people from all walks of life. In fact, the student population is bigger than

◔ There's always time for chatting over coffee

the population of permanent residents, so there is a distinctly young and carefree vibe. Trendy pubs and bars line many squares and the waterfront area is packed with fun-seekers at night. There is almost never any trouble, though; drunk students are a rare sight and there's no serious crime problem.

Culture

Tuscans will tell you that if you want to learn and study Italian, you should do so in Tuscany; this, they assert, is where the real Italian is spoken. Actually, the majority of the history books certainly support the region's linguistic *fons et origo* pedigree. When Italy was unified in 1870, each city-state spoke a different dialect, and it was the language spoken in Tuscany that was chosen as the official Italian tongue.

Much of Pisa's distinct cultural identity was formed from its being a centre of learning, and its famous university complexes and historic academic buildings are known the world over. The city's number-one intellectual pin-up, Galileo Galilei, is its most famous – but by no means only – eminent scholar. Other men of learning – artists, poets and politicians – also helped to enrich Pisa's cultural heritage. Giovanni and Nicola Pisano were the city's greatest sculptors and architects, and wielded massive influence in the Middle Ages (see page 97); you will see their work on show in many historic buildings and churches around the city. This is a city that places great cultural importance in its bricks and mortar, its monuments and buildings. Heavily bombed in World War II, Pisa has rebuilt all of its bridges and most of the waterfront, and new buildings have opened next to the old ones. The city's historical cultural context is very significant and noteworthy events are celebrated in popular street festivals and religious processions, especially in the summer months (see pages 10–13).

But Pisa isn't all about looking back: on a more modern note, one thing you will immediately notice is that many walls are

◆ *Teatro Verdi is the city's main theatre*

⬤ *Detail from the mural* Tuttomondo, *by Keith Haring*

covered with graffiti. Although this does not all fall into the realm of high – or even mid-range – art (or even art), there is one street culture mural that is accepted by all as a piece of real culture, and that's *Tuttomondo* ('The whole world'), the final work by the American street artist Keith Haring, which is found on the exterior back wall of **Chiesa di Sant'Antonio Abate** (ⓐ Piazza Sant'Antonio).

If you're looking for high culture, the **Teatro Verdi** (ⓐ Via Palestro 40 ⓣ (050) 941 111 ⓦ www.teatrodipisa.pi.it) stages ballet as well as opera. You could combine practising your Italian with enjoyment of film at the open-air cinema in **Giardino Scotto** on Lungarno Fibonacci (ⓣ (050) 502 640) during the summer.

Look out for outdoor events like demonstrations, exhibitions, mini markets and children's entertainment – the tourist office (see page 136) will help you discover what's on and how to take part.

⬤ *The Palazzo dell'Orologio was once the seat of the Knights Templar*

Shopping

The historic centre is where the locals go to flash the cash and get drastic with the plastic. Pisa's main shopping area is the pricey but elegant Borgo Stretto, where a vast selection of clothing, jewellery, cosmetics, crafts and book shops line the street. Incidentally, and perhaps slightly more niche, musicians and collectors will be interested in the instrument stores on this street that make violins, violas and cellos. Corso Italia, which runs up to the Ponte di Mezzo, is another popular place to shop, especially if you're looking for chain outlets or cheap Chinese clothes stores. If it's used and vintage clothing you seek, take a bus ride to the resort of Marina di Pisa.

On the second weekend of every month, except during July and August, Pisa becomes a market town. The Piazza dei Cavalieri sells everything from local produce to clothing (and also accommodates antique stalls every second Sunday of the month), while Piazza delle Vettovaglie sells fresh fruit and vegetables in its daily market. Every Wednesday and Saturday, the San Martino district has a great clothing and fashion accessories market.

Large supermarkets and fashion and furnishings outlets are located outside the city walls. The nearest supermarket is **INCOOP** (ⓐ Via Gello ⓣ (050) 830 262), but the reason there aren't many supermarkets dotted about is that Pisans like fresh produce bought daily and cooked the old-fashioned way.

If you want a souvenir to take home that isn't the ubiquitous tacky model of the Leaning Tower, look out for leather goods, alabaster objects, olive oil, wine, and fresh and dried pasta. These are generally made locally. You will see many street

⬥ *Corso Italia is a popular shopping street*

Fabulous food stalls are the norm in Pisa

traders selling bags and fake designer clothing, particularly in
the Campo dei Miracoli, but don't be tempted; it is illegal in Italy
to buy from street traders and if the police see you doing so, you
are liable to pay a fine.

USEFUL SHOPPING PHRASES

What time do the shops open/close?
A che ora aprono/chiudono i negozi?
Ah keh awra ahprawnaw/kewdawnaw ee nehgotsee?

How much is this?
Quant'è?
Kwahnteh?

Can I try this on?
Posso provarlo?
Pawssaw prawvarrlaw?

My size is ...
La mia taglia è ...
Lah meeyah tahlyah eh ...

I'll take this one, thank you
Prenderò questo, grazie
Prehndehroh kwestaw, grahtsyeh

Can you show me the one in the window/this one?
Può mostrarmi quello in vetrina/questo?
Pooh oh mawstrahrmee kwehllaw een vehtreenah/kwehstaw?

This is too large/too small/too expensive
Questo è troppo grande/troppo piccolo/troppo caro
Kwestaw eh tropaw grahndeh/tropaw peekawlaw/
trawpaw kahraw

Eating & drinking

Pisa's restaurateurs are proud of their food, which is simple and wholesome (this, according to local anecdote, is due to the historical Etruscan influence). The only stress you're likely to encounter on Pisa's cuisine scene is an embarrassment of choice: there's a wide range of *osterie*, *trattorie* and restaurants. *Osterie* used to be inns where a traveller could stop to eat, drink and sleep. Today, they are simply eateries decorated in a rustic style and offer large servings of food and local wine at a good price. *Trattorie* tend to be casually furnished, less expensive and family-run, and are consequently ideal for anyone who wants to enjoy local food without spending too much. Wide as the selection of places selling excellent Italian food is, the spectrum could be said to be lacking in two areas: foreign and ethnic restaurants are rare and there are almost no fast-food outlets. Those who would in other cities sink their fangs into bovine burgers have, in Pisa, to eat snacks from cafés and delicatessens.

On the subject of the bovine, Tuscany is famous for its veal, which comes from the Mucca Pisana calves from the nearby rural areas of San Rossore, San Giuliano Terme, Pontasserchio and Migliarino Pisano. Only a small number of restaurants in

PRICE CATEGORIES
Based on a two-course meal for one person, without drinks.
Expect to pay more than stated for fresh fish dishes.
£ up to €20   ££ €20–35   £££ over €35

🔺 Crostini *make for a popular starter*

Pisa are legally able to serve their delicious meat (which is generally referred to as *mucca pisana* on the menu), but do try it if the opportunity arises. Roast mullet, stuffed mussels, squid with potatoes, eel with peas, frogs *alla nonna* (like grandmother makes) and stewed wild boar are other local specialties. San Rossore is renowned for Pecorino cheese, lamb, pine nuts and honey. *Ceci* (chickpeas) are used in many recipes, in particular, *cecina*, a large savoury pancake made with chickpea flour and referred to as *Oro di Pisa*, or 'Pisa's Gold'.

USEFUL DINING PHRASES

I would like a table for ... people
Vorrei un tavolo per ... persone
Vawrray oon tahvawlaw perr ... perrsawneh

Waiter/waitress!
Cameriere/cameriera!
Cahmehryereh/cahmehryera!

May I have the bill, please?
Mi dà il conto, per favore?
Mee dah eel cawntaw, perr fahvawreh?

Could I have it well-cooked/medium/rare please?
Potrei averlo ben cotto/mediamente cotto/al sangue,
per favore?
*Pawtray ahvehrlaw behn cawtaw/mehdeeyahmehnteh
cawtaw/ahl sahngweh, perr fahvawreh?*

I am a vegetarian. Does this contain meat?
Sono vegetariano/vegetariana (fem.). Contiene carne?
*Sawnaw vejetahreeahnaw/vejetahreeahnah.
Contyehneh kahrneh?*

In the autumn there are many exhibitions and food festivals around the hills of Monti Pisani, selling olive oil, mushrooms, chestnuts, vegetables and fresh pasta.

For a starter, or *antipasto*, try *crostini* – little bits of dried bread often served with a chicken liver spread. You could also have the *cacciucco* fish stew, or *bordatino*, a chickpea flour and cabbage recipe that looks like scrambled eggs and tastes delicious. Locals like soup made with mussels, frogs or eels. *Ribollita* is another favourite, a stew concocted with beans, vegetables and leftover bread. Expect a wide variety of main courses from all of Pisa's natural resources: its river, the sea, the hills and the land. Sweets include Pisan chestnut cake and *pan ficato* (fig cake). You'll find interesting flavours of ice cream for sale at the area's *gelaterie*. From the hills around Pisa, particularly Palaia and Lari, you can get delicious cherries in season.

White wine is produced locally, primarily from Trebbiano and Malvasia grapes, while red wines are produced using Trebbiano Toscano, Sangiovese and Malvasia del Chianti grapes. Look for the word 'DOC' on the wine bottle, which stands for *Denominazione d'Origine Controllata* and guarantees that wine meets a local standard in terms of having been produced from certain grape types and soil (but makes no claims to guarantee quality). Other wines from the region include Chianti Colline Pisane, Bianco Pisano di San Torpè and Montescudaio.

Italians like to sit down and enjoy their food, so expect lunchtimes to be long. Many shops and businesses close for lunch and don't open until at least two hours later. It seems old traditions die hard in Pisa when it comes to food and drink.

Entertainment & nightlife

Pisa may not exactly be Las Vegas, but you can have a great time here. The city's nightlife is generally animated by the large student population, and at its geographical heart is the historic centre, which throbs with bars and restaurants that teem with academics, locals and tourists. Tables spill into the streets and squares in summer and music bellows from the surrounding pubs and bars. The Pisan nightlife scene is not characterised by a cool and exclusive lifestyle pose but by a warm and inclusive invitation to join in and have fun.

Friday night is when the students like to go out (Saturday night tending to be devoted to homework and studying), and a popular gathering point for locals is the historic Ponte di Mezzo, so if you swing by the bridge you should easily be able to join a local group of fun-lovers.

Dance halls, clubs and discos can be found on Marina di Pisa, a cornucopia of beach life entertainment possibilities that's a short car or bus ride away from the city centre. A couple of the clubs offer live music, including jazz nights; these aren't easy to find as they tend to be down backstreets, so make friends with the locals.

Theatre-goers will be intrigued by two quite distinct dramatic outlets. **Teatro Sant'Andrea** (ⓐ Via del Cuore) is a fabulous place to catch the work of young, up-and-coming writers and performers, while showbiz city central is undoubtedly Teatro Verdi (see page 82), where the fare ranges from heavy classics to lightweight froth.

CARNIVAL

In this part of the world, carnivals are key entertainment vehicles. February is carnival time, and Pisans who know a good knees-up when they see one tend to flock to the seaside town of Viareggio, whose offering is reckoned to be second in Italy only to that of Venice. The carnival takes place on the Sunday before Mardi Gras and is typified by hundreds of colourful floats cruising down the streets as people in elaborate costumes and masks dance and have fun. There are prizes for the best float and the chance to be crowned as 'Miss Viareggio Carnival', a beauty and talent contest that predates *The X Factor* by several hundred years.

The carnival's theme changes every year but always accommodates large portions of glitz and glamour. And the happy, relaxed ambience remains the same. Various masked balls also take place during the evening. If that's a little too *Eyes Wide Shut* for you, check what's happening in the local discos and clubs – most join in the festive spirit with a buffet and special drinks offers.

If you aren't visiting Pisa during carnival time but are interested in socio-historical aspects of the subject, do visit the **Museo della Cittadella del Carnevale** (ⓐ Via Santa Maria Goretti, Viareggio ⓣ (0584) 530 48 ⓦ www.viareggio.ilcarnevale.com).

Sport & relaxation

SPECTATOR SPORTS
Football
Known to local fans as 'the jigsaws', because they always fall apart in the box, the not-very-mighty **Pisa Calcio** (ⓦ www.pisacalcio.it) are currently loitering in Serie B, but they do play at the impressive **Arena Garibaldi – Stadio Romeo Anconetani** (ⓦ www.pisacalcio.it/stadio).

Horse racing
For those who feel that the detachment of a flutter in euros will numb the pain of financial bereavement, the **Ippodromo San Rossore** (ⓐ Via della Sterpaia 1 ⓣ 050 526 11 ⓦ www.sanrossore.it)

△ *The Cosmopolitan Golf Club in Tirrenia also has an enormous swimming pool*

is a superb venue for enjoying equine endeavours. The complex consists of 10,000 covered and open seats, a hurdle course, steeple chase, betting areas and a restaurant.

PARTICIPATION SPORTS
Bird watching

Twitchers should don their binoculars and head along Lungarno Galilei and Lungarno Fibonacci, following the path along the river Arno. No fewer than 64 species of birds have been sighted here. ⓐ Piagge

Golf

The **Cosmopolitan Golf Club** (ⓐ Viale Pisorno 60, Tirrenia ⓣ (050) 336 33 ⓦ www.golftirrenia.it ⓝ Bus: CPT Line 010) in Tirrenia is a short distance from Pisa on the SS1 road. There's an 18-hole golf course, driving range, golf bag hire, private lessons as well as a swimming pool, beach, restaurant and residence.

Swimming

The nearest public swimming pool is in La Gabella in Calci. ⓐ Via Lungomonte 41 ⓣ (050) 938 720 ⓦ www.nuotolagabella.it ⓛ 09.00–16.00, 19.00–22.00 Mon–Fri ⓝ Bus: CPT Lines 120, 160

RELAXATION

Bagni di Pisa This stylish spa in the district of San Giuliano Terme (see page 109) offers an array of ways to be pampered: there are thermal water pools and a restaurant, a hammam, beauty treatments, specialist consultations, skin care master classes and, of course, massage.

Accommodation

There's a wide selection of accommodation options in Pisa, from B&Bs and farmhouses to stately homes. Bed and breakfast places are mostly simply furnished but immaculately clean, and the owners are usually happy to help tourists get to know the city.

Some of the really good options are out of town, offering activities like swimming, wine tasting and horse riding; these may be considerably cheaper than city-centre options and are certainly worth checking out. Many of Pisa's hotels are set in historic buildings, so the rooms may be small but they don't fall short when it comes to elegance. If you want to splash out on something special, stay in one of several large stately homes that are now open as hotels. These are generally set in the countryside, with lovely private gardens where you can sit and take tea or just rest and relax. Whatever you do, don't cruise the streets of Pisa in your car looking for vacancies, as the historic centre is strictly out of bounds to cars without a permit.

In summer and at the times of popular festivals (see pages 10–13), you would do well to book accommodation at least a month in advance. Camping and hotels on Marina di Pisa may be easier to find on the spur of the moment.

PRICE CATEGORIES
Ratings are based on the average price per night of a room for two people with breakfast.
£ up to €100   **££** €100–200   **£££** over €200

HOTELS

Hotel Astor £ Nice 2-star hotel in a quiet location, with modern décor and an offbeat snack bar downstairs that serves cocktails and aperitifs. The really good news is that it's within walking distance of the Leaning Tower. ⓐ Via Alessandro Manzoni 22 (Campo dei Miracoli & Santa Maria Quarter) ⓣ (050) 445 51 ⓦ www.hotelastor.pisa.it ⓝ Bus: LAM Rossa

Hotel Roseto £ Right in the city centre, this budget hotel has none of the drawbacks that that term implies. The staff are very courteous and the size and décor of the rooms belie their price. ⓐ Via Mascagni 24 (Over the bridges) ⓣ (050) 425 96 ⓦ www.hotelroseto.it ⓝ Bus: LAM Rossa

Hotel Francesco £–££ A 3-star hotel that has recently been modernised, just a stone's throw from the Leaning Tower. You can rent bikes and scooters through the hotel (see website for details). ⓐ Via Santa Maria 129 (Campo dei Miracoli & Santa Maria Quarter) ⓣ (050) 555 453 ⓦ www.hotelfrancesco.com ⓝ Bus: 4

Grand Hotel Bonanno ££ Newly built 89-room hotel with all the expected comforts and a restaurant. Parking is available. It's located near the San Rossore train station. ⓐ Via Carlo Francesco Gabba 17 (Campo dei Miracoli & Santa Maria Quarter) ⓣ (050) 524 030 ⓦ www.grandhotelbonanno.it ⓝ Bus: 5

Hotel Bologna ££ A 4-star, friendly, well organised and comfortable hotel in a quiet location. Another spot that's within walking distance of the train station and Leaning Tower. A big plus is that there are beautifully painted frescoes by Maurizio Magretti in the breakfast room, depicting the tower houses along the waterfront. Aperitifs are served at 16.00 every day. Internet access and courtesy coaches are also available. ⓐ Via Mazzini 57 (Campo dei Miracoli & Santa Maria Quarter) ⓣ (050) 502 120 ⓦ www.hotelbologna.pisa.it ⓝ Bus: LAM Rossa

Hotel La Pace ££ This 3-star hotel is located very near the central rail station in an arcade. Rooms are beautifully decorated and, if you're feeling homesick, nostalgic or both, you can make a phone call from a red English telephone box that sits in the reception area. ⓐ Viale Gramsci 55 (Over the bridges) ⓣ (050) 293 51 ⓦ www.hotellapace.it ⓝ Bus: LAM Rossa

Hotel Victoria ££ The oldest hotel in Pisa boasts an impressive list of influential past guests, including royalty from all over the world.

The rooms are fabulously furnished and elegant. ⓐ Lungarno Pacinotti 12 (Campo dei Miracoli & Santa Maria Quarter) ⓣ (050) 940 111 ⓦ www.royalvictoria.it ⓝ Bus: LAM Rossa; LAM Verde

Hotel Relais dell'Orologio £££ This 5-star listed building was restored under the supervision of the Department of Monuments

🔺 *Hotel Relais dell'Orologio's garden*

and Fine Arts, so it's no wonder that it's an aesthetic delight. The compact rooms have beamed ceilings and immaculately soft fine furnishings. There's a romantic garden at the rear in which to take breakfast or enjoy a cup of tea. ⓐ Via della Faggiola 12–14 (Campo dei Miracoli & Santa Maria Quarter) ① (050) 830 361 ⓦ www.hotelrelaisorologio.com ⓝ Bus: 4

BED & BREAKFAST

B&B Santa Chiara £ A totally restructured apartment near the Santa Chiara hospital, with four rooms and en suite bathrooms. ⓐ Via Derna 27 (Campo dei Miracoli & Santa Maria Quarter) ① (050) 407 20 ⓦ www.bbsantachiara.it ⓝ Bus: 4

Casa Aruna £ An artist's den of simplicity and cleanliness. This B&B has three rooms and two bathrooms. ⓐ Via Santa Apollonia 7 (Centre of Town & San Francesco Quarter) ① Mobile: 333 4629 065 ⓦ http://utenti.lycos.it/aruna ⓝ Bus: 4

Relais dell'Ussero £ A four-bedroomed B&B apartment, with breakfast offered downstairs at the Caffè dell'Ussero (see page 85). ⓐ Lungarno Pacinotti (Campo dei Miracoli & Santa Maria Quarter) ① (050) 575 428 ⓦ www.ussero.com ⓝ Bus: LAM Rossa; LAM Verde

CAMPING

Campeggio Internazionale £ Bungalows, campervans and tents are all welcome here. There's a children's play area and private beach. ⓐ Via Litoranea 7 (Campo dei Miracoli & Santa Maria Quarter) ① (050) 352 11 ⓦ www.campeggiointernazionale.com ⓝ Bus: CPT Line 010

THE BEST OF PISA

Mention Pisa and the Leaning Tower is the first thing that pops into one's mind. But just walk along the river Arno, cross the bridges and you'll discover a wealth of history, architecture and culture. Then there's the natural beauty of its green spaces, which will enthral you and the gregariousness of its inhabitants, which will charm you.

TOP 10 ATTRACTIONS

- **Torre Pendente (Leaning Tower)** A tipsy-looking architectural mishap that made Pisa famous (see page 67)

- **Duomo (Cathedral)** The oldest of the buildings in the Campo dei Miracoli and a triumph of the Pisan Romanesque style (see page 66)

- **Battistero di San Giovanni (Baptistery)** Ennobled by Nicola Pisano's pulpit, it's big but not brassy and has fabulous acoustics (see page 58)

- **Camposanto (Cemetery)** Another Campo dei Miracoli gem that's said to be the loveliest cemetery in the world (see page 62)

- **Chiesa di Santa Maria della Spina (Church of Santa Maria of the Thorn)** A gorgeous Gothic church with a fascinating story to tell (see page 95)

- **Parco Naturale di San Rossore (San Rossore park)** Just a stroll will transport you from city vibe to natural chill-out. Pack a picnic and spend the day there (see page 63)

- **Arsenale** A Medici ships' graveyard that's still being excavated and is uncovering objects of total fascination (see page 74)

- **Orto Botanico (Botanic Garden)** Browse around and check out the rare varieties of plants and flowers in this hothouse of horticultural delights (see page 68)

- **Basilica di San Piero a Grado** An amazing circular stone-walled cathedral. Inside there are murals and exciting excavations (see page 58)

- **Caffè dell'Ussero** With its beautiful red-brick façade, this historic coffee house has been accommodating Europe's intellectuals for over 200 years (see page 85)

◗ *Amazing architecture clustered together on the Campo dei Miracoli*

Suggested itineraries

HALF-DAY: PISA IN A HURRY

Stay within the Campo dei Miracoli and visit the Leaning Tower (see page 67), the baptistery (see page 58) and the cathedral (see page 66). If you have time, walk down Via Santa Maria to browse around the shops.

1 DAY: TIME TO SEE A LITTLE MORE

Walk up Corso Italia to do some window shopping until you reach the Ponte di Mezzo bridge. Cross it, stroll around the Borgo Stretto medieval quarter and walk as far as Piazza dei Cavalieri for lunch. After lunch, head for Piazza Cavalotti – from here you'll find yourself in the middle of Via Santa Maria. Then hit Campo dei Miracoli to soak up its manifold marvels.

2–3 DAYS: TIME TO SEE MUCH MORE

After treating yourself to full immersion in Campo dei Miracoli, spend an afternoon in the Botanic Garden (see page 66). Having more time to play with gives you the chance to get out of town for a bit. You can relax by playing golf in Tirrenia (see page 35) or really relax by being pampered in the San Giuliano Terme spa (see page 109).

LONGER: ENJOYING PISA TO THE FULL

Check out the historic churches dotted around the city and stroll along the popular shopping streets and arcades. The San Rossore park (see page 63) provides many sporting activities, with guided activities such as trekking, cycling and horse riding.

You could explore the Etruscan village of Volterra (see page 116) then head to the hills to admire the Tuscan countryside, stopping off at Calci (see page 104) and Vicopisano (see page 110).

◯ *The Botanic Garden hosts rare varieties of plants and flowers*

Something for nothing

You don't have to spend a lot of money to have a good time in Pisa. Just walking around the Campo dei Miracoli (see page 58) is priceless, and you can admire the heights of human achievement without plumbing the depths of bankruptcy. Within the city boundaries, there's a lovely walk in the Giardino Scotto park on Lungarno Fibonacci, with a splendid view of the river from the wall of the Fortezza. Entrance to the park of San Rossore (see page 63) is also free. Just a brief stroll to admire the grounds among the trees and flowers will send you into realms bucolic, and you may like to pack a picnic and even spend the day there. Alternatively, take the bus to the Marina di Pisa and promenade along its glorious seafront.

Churches are normally free to poke around in Pisa, which must be one of Europe's most ecclesiastically rich cities. Highly recommended is the Chiesa di San Sisto (see page 64), where medieval boats are hung on the walls in the corner and there's a display of Pisan flags; Santa Chiara (see page 64) is impressive, as it holds a thorn that was reputedly from Christ's crucifixion crown; Pisa's other leaning tower is adjoined to Chiesa di San Nicola (see page 63) and the white marble façade of the Santa Caterina is infinitely admirable (see page 64).

If you're interested in Galileo, visit the free **Domus Galileiana** (ⓐ Via Santa Maria 26 ⓣ (050) 237 26) that has manuscripts, books, autographs and other documents on show that relate to his experiments and work.

If you are in Pisa on the second or fourth Sunday of the month you'll be able to browse at your leisure over the market stalls that dot the city centre and display arts and crafts, vintage clothing and collectables.

🔺 *Marina di Pisa and the seafront are just ten minutes by road from the city*

When it rains

Unfortunately, most of Pisa's attractions or monuments are in the open air – if it does rain, the best plan may simply be to get yourself a big umbrella and get on with it. If it rains a lot, a stroll along Borgo Stretto's arcaded shops is a nice, dry option. You can also visit the Museo Nazionale di San Matteo (see page 81), which flipped from being a convent of Benedict nuns to a new life as a prison. After World War II, it became one of the most important museums in Italy, with collections of paintings, ceramics and religious artefacts. On the subject of things religious, you can always avoid inclement weather by spending time in any of the city's glorious churches. A glimpse at the beauty within will make you glad it rained. Back under that umbrella, splash down to Lungarno Pacinotti to the Palazzo Reale (see page 70). The former residence of the Medici family houses a grand collection of art and royal furnishings and you'll have a good two hours here to dry off.

Then, nip over the Ponte di Mezzo to see Palazzo Blu (see page 97). Recently opened in its new guise as a temple to the arts and culture, this ex-home of the Counts Giuli has an unmissable bright blue façade. It's worth a visit just to see the splendidly decorated rooms with restored frescoes, furnishings and paintings by numerous Italian artists.

If you prefer not to walk between museums in the rain, you could take a short bus ride to Calci to visit the Natural History Museum (see page 104), which is being continuously renovated and updated. It is owned by the University of Pisa and houses life-sized replicas of dinosaurs; the mythological creatures and

🔺 *Palazzo Reale has a great collection of art*

the little aquarium at the end of the visit are particularly interesting for children. Here you'll also find an old monastery that still has little rooms where the priests and friars dwelt.

On arrival

TIME DIFFERENCE

Pisa is on Central European Time, one hour ahead of Greenwich Mean Time. Daylight saving applies: clocks go forward one hour at the end of March and back one hour at the end of October, at the same time as in the UK.

ARRIVING

By air

Galileo Galilei airport (ⓣ (050) 500 707 or (050) 849 300 ⓦ www.pisa-airport.com) is 2 km (just over a mile) north of Pisa town centre. The airport is the busiest in Tuscany and has all the usual facilities, including car rental offices (see page 56). Regular buses to the city centre leave from outside the airport, with a journey time of just ten minutes. LAM Rossa, LAM Verde and **Compagnia Pisana Trasporti** (CPT, ⓦ www.cpt.pisa.it) buses go to the centre. There are hourly trains to Pisa central station from the airport's rail terminal. Alternatively, you can plump for a short ride in a taxi.

By rail

There are two railway stations in the city: **Pisa Centrale** and **Pisa San Rossore** (see ⓦ www.ferroviedellostato.it for both). Pisa Centrale station has toilets, a bar and fast food restaurant, a newspaper stand and a taxi stand just outside. The LAM Rossa bus travels directly from here to the Campo dei Miracoli and the city centre. San Rossore train station isn't so well equipped, but is under development and has the advantage of being close to the Campo dei Miracoli – get off here for the Leaning Tower and follow the road leading out from the underpass.

By road

If you are driving from Florence, Rome or Bologna, you will arrive on the A11 motorway. Exit at Pisa Nord, then take SS1 Aurelia going south. From Genoa, take the A12 motorway and exit at Pisa Nord or Pisa Centro. Motorway tolls apply. Note that the historic centre of Pisa has restricted access for cars so you will not be able to drive around here.

The city's main bus station is on Piazza Vittorio Emanuele in the San Antonio district. Buses for out of town destinations leave from Piazza Vittorio Emanuele bus station, while the hub for city buses is at Pisa Centrale railway station.

⬧ Pisa Centrale, the main railway station

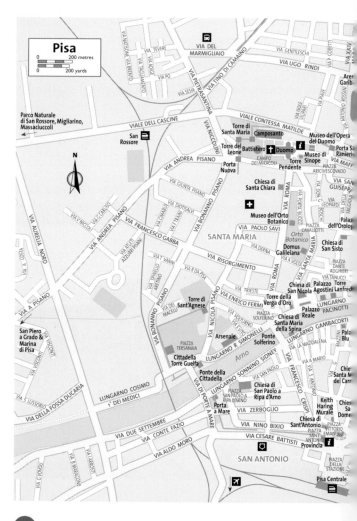

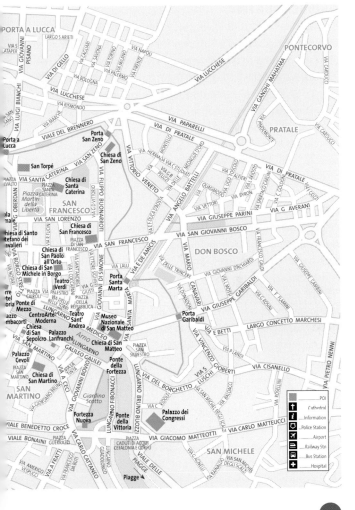

FINDING YOUR FEET

Pisa is an easy city to find your way around. Take care when crossing the roads and going over the bridges. Cars don't often stop and do tend to drive on even if you are trying to cross the road. Beware of the 'little green man' sign indicating you can cross: this is regarded with derision by some drivers. Cars may also come out of side streets unexpectedly. The town centre is crowded with students at night and pickpockets operate in the Campo dei Miracoli, so make sure your personal belongings are safe. Put your bag over your chest or under your coat. You should also avoid the station area at night.

ORIENTATION

Pisa is small, square and easy to navigate around. The river Arno cuts through the middle, and its name is the origin of a local oddity in addresses: you'll often see the word 'Lungarno', which literally means 'along the River Arno', but should be regarded as 'Riverbank'. The area north of the river is known as the Tramontana district, and the one south of the river is called Mezzogiorno. Starting from the Campo dei Miracoli in the northwest and walking southeast, you will come to the centre of town, Via Santa Maria. Carry on along the waterfront and the medieval Borgo Stretto district and cross the river and you'll arrive at Pisa's central train station.

GETTING AROUND

The best way to get around Pisa is on foot. However, there are good bus services in the city, details of whose connections we have listed where they present a practical alternative to walking.

IF YOU GET LOST, TRY ...

Excuse me, do you speak English?
Mi scusi, parla inglese?
Mee scoozee, parrla eenglehzeh?

Excuse me, is this the right way to the old town/the city centre/the tourist office/the station/the bus station?
Mi scusi, è questa la strada per città vecchia/al centro città/l'ufficio informazioni turistiche/alla stazione ferroviaria/alla stazione degli autobus?
Mee scoozee, eh kwehstah lah strahda perr lah cheetta vehkyah/ahl chentraw cheetteh/looffeechaw eenforrmahtsyawnee tooreesteekeh/ahlla stahtsyawneh ferrawvyarya/ahlla stahtsyawneh delee aowtoboos?

The LAM Verde and LAM Rossa bus services stop at all districts in the town; tickets can be bought from newspaper kiosks or *tabacchi* (tobacconists) and are valid for an hour's travel. Stamp your ticket when you get on the bus. The website for LAM Verde, LAM Rossa and the CPT (Compagnia Pisana Transporti) numbered buses is Ⓦ www.cpt.pisa.it

If you need a taxi, call **Radio Taxi** (Ⓣ (050) 541 600 Ⓦ www.cotapi.it).

CAR HIRE
You may not drive in the city centre, so it's only a good idea to

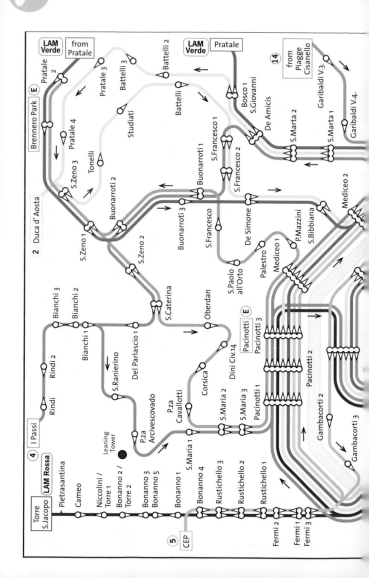

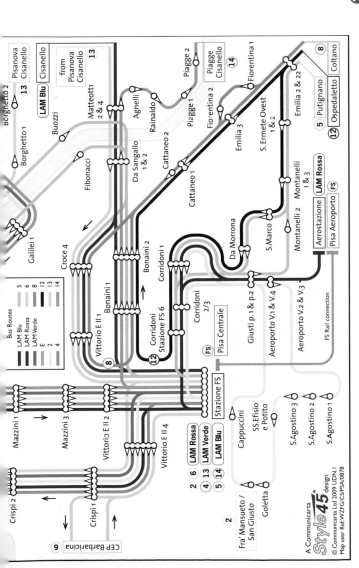

PARKING

You'll find a free car park on the northern outskirts of the city, just 800 m (956 yards) from the Campo dei Miracoli. There are good facilities here, including toilets, a bar, a petrol station and a hotel reservation office. Just outside the city walls through Porta San Zeno on Via Paparelli is a free park. From here, park and ride buses go directly to the city centre and the waterfront. There's no parking on Wednesdays and Saturdays because of street markets. All in all, it's best to leave your car outside the city as fines are frequent and expensive.

hire a car if you want to see destinations outside of Pisa. The best place to pick up a car is at the airport (see page 48). Check that the insurance documents are in order before driving away.

Reputable hire companies with offices at the airport are:

Autoeuropa ❶ (050) 506 883 Ⓦ www.autoeuropa.it

Avis ❶ (050) 420 28 Ⓦ www.avisautonoleggio.it

Europcar ❶ (050) 410 81 Ⓦ www.europcar.com

Sixt ❶ (050) 462 09 Ⓦ www.sixt.it

● *Pisa's Cathedral is said to represent life*

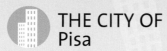

THE CITY OF
Pisa

Campo dei Miracoli & Santa Maria Quarter

This north-of-the-river quarter covers a triangular area, with Campo dei Miracoli – laid out in the fourth century as the city's religious focal point and still inspiring awe today – in the north, Citadella Torre Guelfa in the southwest and Teatro Verdi in the southeast. It is Pisa's main tourist area, and the easiest way to get around is on foot; although public transport details are given here for some sights, do yourself a favour – walk. Seeing them whizz past from a bus window would almost qualify as self-harming. If you're planning on visiting a lot of the sights, it makes sense to save money by getting a combined ticket for the Camposanto cemetery, the Museo dell' Opera del Duomo and Museo delle Sinopie (the ticket is available from any of those places).

SIGHTS & ATTRACTIONS

Basilica di San Piero a Grado

This tenth-century basilica, which is also known as Basilica di San Pietro Apostolo, was built on top of the foundations of at least two ancient churches whose remains are clearly visible from the inside. Its main point of interest is its partially Gothic interior, which includes some amazingly ambitious religiously themed medieval frescoes. ⓐ Via Vecchia di Marina 5, San Piero a Grado ⓣ (050) 960 065 ⓛ 08.00–19.00 ⓝ Bus: CPT Line 010

Battistero di San Giovanni (Baptistery)

This dome-shaped chapel has four entrances, a slight lean, and

◆ *Pisa's Baptistery represents birth*

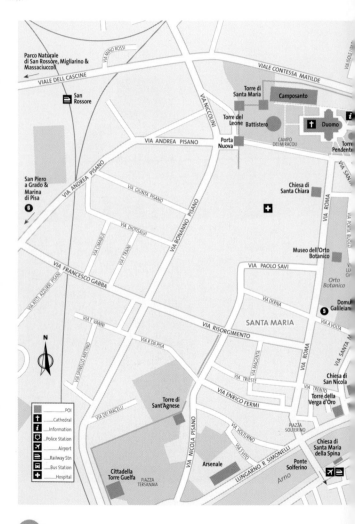

Parco Naturale di San Rossòre, Migliarino & Massaciuccoli

VIA NINO ROSSI

VIALE CONTESSA MATILDE

VIALE DELL CASCINE

San Rossore

VIA NICOLINI

Torre di Santa Maria

Camposanto

Torre del Leone

Battistero

Porta Nuova

CAMPO DEI MIRACOLI

Duomo

Torre Pendente

VIA ANDREA PISANO

San Piero a Grado & Marina di Pisa

VIA ANDREA PISANO

VIA GIUNTA PISANO

VIA BONANNO PISANO

Chiesa di Santa Chiara

VIA ROMA

VIA SANT

VIA PORTA BUOZZI

VIA DIOTISALVI

VIA CIMABUE

VIA T. PRINI

Museo dell'Orto Botanico

VIA FRANCESCO GABBA

VIA PAOLO SAVI

Orto Botanico

VIA ARTU AZZURRI PISANI

VIA DERNA

Domus Galileiana

VIA A VOLTA

VIA T. VANNI

VIA RISORGIMENTO

SANTA MARIA

N

VIA SPINELLO ARETINO

VIA R DA PISA

VIA ROMA

VIA SANTA

VIA MAGENTA

VIA TRIESTE

Chiesa di San Nicola

VIA TRENTO

Torre della Verga d'Oro

Torre di Sant'Agnese

VIA ENRICO FERMI

PIAZZA SOLFERINO

Chiesa di Santa Maria della Spina

VIA DEI MACELLI

VIA VOLTURNO

VIA SITO

LUNGARNO R. SIMONELLI

Ponte Solferino

Arno

VIA NICOLA PISANO

Cittadella Torre Guelfa

PIAZZA TERSANAIA

Arsenale

	POI
✝	Cathedral
i	Information
⊙	Police Station
✈	Airport
⊠	Railway Stn
⊟	Bus Station
✚	Hospital

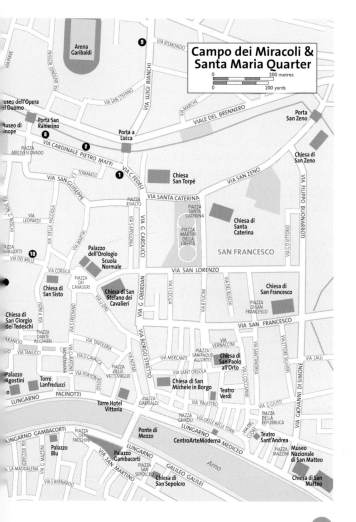

Campo dei Miracoli & Santa Maria Quarter

0   200 metres
0   200 yards

Arena Garibaldi

Museo dell'Opera del Duomo

Museo di Sinope

Porta San Ranierino

Porta a Lucca

Porta San Zeno

Chiesa di San Zeno

PIAZZA ARICIVESCOVADO

Chiesa San Torpé

Chiesa di Santa Caterina

PIAZZA RIVALTO

PIAZZA SANTA CATERINA

PIAZZA MARTIRI DELLA LIBERTA

SAN FRANCESCO

PIAZZA CAVALLOTTI

Palazzo dell'Orologio Scuola Normale

PIAZZA DEI CAVALIERI

Chiesa di San Sisto

Chiesa di San Stefano dei Cavalieri

Chiesa di San Francesco

PIAZZA DI SAN FRANCESCO

Chiesa di San Giorgio dei Tedeschi

PIAZZA DANTE ALIGHIERI

Palazzo Agostini

Torre Lanfreducci

PIAZZA DELLE VETTOVAGLIE

PIAZZA SAN PAOLO ALL'ORTO

Chiesa di San Paolo all'Orto

Chiesa di San Michele in Borgo

Teatro Verdi

Torre Hotel Vittoria

PIAZZA GARIBALDI

PIAZZA CAIRDLI

Ponte di Mezzo

CentroArteModerna

Teatro Sant'Andrea

PIAZZA DELLA REPUBBLICA

Museo Nazionale di San Matteo

Palazzo Blu

PIAZZA DEI FACCHINI

Palazzo Gambacorti

PIAZZA SAN SEPOLCRO

Chiesa di San Sepolcro

Arno

Chiesa di San Matteo

incredible acoustics. Since being completed in 1260, it has been of enormous significance to the city. Indeed, for many years, citizens first had to be baptised here before being able to go and pray in the Duomo. Its original architect, Diotisalvi, died long before the building was finished, and the project was handed over to local superstar Nicola Pisano (see page 97), who added his own ideas to the mix, notably the astonishing marble pulpit that shows vignettes from the life of Christ. ⓐ Campo dei Miracoli ⓣ (050) 560 547 ⓦ www.opapisa.it ⓛ 10.00–17.00 Nov–Feb (09.00–18.00 25 Dec–7 Jan); 09.00–18.00 1 Mar–13 Mar; 09.00–19.00 14 Mar–20 Mar & Oct; 08.00–20.00 21 Mar–Sept; ⓝ Bus: LAM Rossa. Admission charge

Camposanto (Cemetery)

This celebrated cemetery is said to have been built using sacred soil brought from the Holy Land. Until World War II, its intricate Roman tombs were surrounded by frescoed walls. Bomb damage affected the walls terribly, but a huge renovation programme is now in progress. ⓐ Campo dei Miracoli ⓣ (050) 560 547 ⓦ www.opapisa.it ⓛ 10.00–17.00 Nov–Feb (09.00–18.00 25 Dec–7 Jan); 09.00–18.00 1 Mar–13 Mar & Oct; 09.00–19.00 14 Mar–20 Mar; 08.00–20.00 21 Mar–Sept ⓝ Bus: LAM Rossa. Admission charge

Chiesa di San Giorgio dei Tedeschi

This church's interest is principally anecdotal. Built in 1317, it was named after the German mercenaries who fought in the battle of Montecatini. Originally it was an *ospizio dei trovatelli*, or orphans' hospital. Its door once had a wheel attached to it and parents used to strap unwanted children on it so that they could be abandoned

SAN ROSSORE PARK

Officially known as the **Parco Naturale di San Rossore, Migliarino and Massaciuccoli** (ⓦ www.parks.it/parco.migliarino.san.rossore), this wonderful park stretches as far as Viareggio and Livorno. There are 23 hectares (57 acres) of unspoiled habitat of forests, sandy shores and inland marshes, with animals roaming free. Sporting activities take place daily – check at the **visitor centre** (ⓐ Villa Medicea, Via di Palazzi 21, Coltano ⓣ (050) 989 084), which is open all year round.

Of special interest here is Lake Massaciuccoli, also known as the Lake of Puccini, where you can visit **Puccini's house and grave** (ⓦ www.fondazionesimonettapuccini.it). There's also a children's park and boat trips in the summer months (ⓣ (0548) 350 424). All in all, fabulous for the family.

with full anonymity. The church is not open to the public.
ⓐ Via Santa Maria ⓝ Bus: 4, 21

Chiesa di San Nicola

Although its interior contains some fabulous religious paintings, this church's main claim to fame is that it has Pisa's second-most famous leaning tower (but as it is cemented in between two other buildings, it's unlikely that it will totter any more than it has done already). The Romanesque bell tower was built by Mr Campo dei Miracoli, the architect Diotisalvi. ⓐ Via Santa Maria 2 ⓣ (050) 246 77 ⓛ 11.00–13.00 ⓝ Bus: 4, 21

Chiesa di San Sisto

Completed in 1133, this medieval stone structure is a great example of the Pisan Romanesque style. The relative modesty of its interior illustrates Pisa's unbelievable wealth of ecclesiastical beauty: its simple elegance seems, in the context of the other churches here, to be almost tedious; in most other cities, it would be a stand-out sight. ⓐ Via Corsica ⓣ (050) 482 90 ⓛ 09.00–12.00 ⓝ Bus: 4

Chiesa di Santa Caterina

Another example of Pisan Romanesque, though the upper sections are Gothic. There's a distinctive delicate rose marble window and some statues by yet another Pisano, Nino. ⓐ Via Santa Caterina ⓣ (050) 552 883 ⓛ 15.30–18.00 ⓝ Bus: 4

Chiesa di Santa Chiara

A one-time hospital chapel whose frankly dull architecture is obliterated by the claim that it contains a sacred thorn from Christ's crucifixion garland, carefully guarded and on show inside. ⓐ Via Roma ⓛ 09.00–19.00 ⓝ Bus: 4, 21

Cittadella Vecchia & Torre Guelfa

The cittadella and tower were once part of the shipyards' defensive wall. Recent restoration has given public access to the tower, where an exhibition of prominent coats of arms from Florentine captains is on show. ⓐ Piazza Tersanaia ⓣ (050) 321 5446 ⓦ www.comune.pisa.it ⓛ 15.00–19.00 Fri–Sun; 10.00–13.00, 15.00–17.00 second Sun of month ⓝ Bus: 6, 21. Admission charge

City Wall

Dating back to the 12th century, the 7 km (4 mile) fortified city wall was built to protect the maritime republic. Nowadays, people use the adjoining cycle path or bravely walk along the wall with

⬤ *The Torre Guelfa is part of the city's defensive walls*

their dogs. A short stretch of the wall near the Camposanto cemetery, including the Tower of Santa Maria, is open to the public. Bus: LAM Rossa

Duomo (Cathedral)

Shaped like the Christian cross with 68 columns, Pisa's cathedral has three naved transepts and some Byzantine mosaics. The gilded ceiling was restored by the Medici family, whose coat of arms is shown there. The remains of Saint Ranieri are laid to rest here and Galileo is said to have formulated his theory on the pendulum movement by watching the incense lamp in the middle of the cathedral. The original lamp is kept in the Camposanto. Campo dei Miracoli (050) 560 547 www.opapisa.it 10.00–17.00 Nov–Feb (09.00–18.00 25 Dec–7 Jan); 09.00–18.00 1 Mar–13 Mar; 09.00–19.00 14 Mar–20 Mar & Oct; 08.00–20.00 21 Mar–Sept Bus: LAM Rossa. Admission charge

Orto Botanico (Botanic Garden)

The Orto Botanico dates back to 1544 and is the oldest botanical garden in Europe. It is also among the most beautiful. Two of the oldest trees, a magnolia and a ginkgo biloba, planted in 1787, are to be found in the cedar section. Many ponds adorn the gardens, and there are eight fountains and greenhouses bursting with exotic flowers. Plants from ancient Egypt once used for medicinal and culinary purposes are grown and tested here. The Botany Institute in the grounds dates from 1591 and has a façade of ornamental seashells. Via Luca Ghini 5 (050) 221 1313 www.biologia.unipi.it/ortobotanico 08.30–17.00 Mon–Fri, 08.30–13.00 Sat Bus: 4, 21. Admission charge

Torre Pendente (Leaning Tower)

Pisa's Torre Pendente is unique and strangely magnificent. The freestanding bell tower, which was designed to be part of the Duomo and has eight floors and seven bells, was, not surprisingly, designed to stand vertically. However, thanks to the Campo dei Miracoli's sandy subsoil, it started to lean almost the minute construction began in 1173. Pluckily, it was decided to carry on regardless. The second architect, Bonnano Pisano, tried to

⏷ *Probably the most unique bell tower in the world*

straighten the tower by making the columns on the third floor longer but wasn't entirely successful, so everybody decided to ignore the problem and construction was completed in 1360. In 1990 the bells were removed and the tower was closed to the public as earth was siphoned out and the lean factor was reduced by 17 cm (7 inches). It was re-opened to the public in 2001. Some 294 steps lead to the top of the bell tower and a maximum of 40 people only are allowed to mount the tower every thirty minutes, so make sure you buy your tickets at least 15 days in advance or you will not be able to climb it. ⓐ Campo dei Miracoli ⓣ (050) 560 547 ⓦ www.latorrependente.it ⓛ 10.00–17.00 Nov–Feb (09.00–18.00 25 Dec–7 Jan); 09.00–18.00 1 Mar–13 Mar; 09.00–19.00 14 Mar–20 Mar & Oct; 08.00–20.00 21 Mar–Sept ⓝ Bus: LAM Rossa. Admission charge ⓘ Tickets can be purchased online until 15 days before your visit via ⓦ www.opapisa.it

CULTURE

Museo dell' Opera del Duomo

This is a must for sculpture fans as it's a sort of repository for the city's great works. Many of the original pieces from monuments that have at one time or another adorned the Campo dei Miracoli are kept here for preservation purposes, alongside exhibits that are originally from the Duomo. This represents a fabulous opportunity to get up close and personal to some real works of art. ⓐ Campo dei Miracoli ⓣ (050) 560 547 ⓦ www.opapisa.it ⓛ 10.00–17.00 Nov–Feb (09.00–18.00 25 Dec–7 Jan); 09.00–18.00 1 Mar–13 Mar; 09.00–19.00 14 Mar–20 Mar & Oct; 08.00–20.00 21 Mar–Sept ⓝ Bus: LAM Rossa. Admission charge

🔺 *Museo dell'Opera del Duomo has original pieces from the Field monuments*

Museo delle Sinopie

A sinope is a red powdered drawing that is fixed to the wall and used to outline a fresco. This museum shows how the process works and how frescoes are taken down to be restored. Intriguingly, it contains the original plans for the fresco ornamentation of Camposanto cemetery, which became invaluable when the frescoes themselves fell victim to bombing in World War II. ⓐ Campo dei Miracoli ☎ (050) 560 547 ◷ 10.00–17.00 Nov–Feb (09.00–18.00 25 Dec–7 Jan); 09.00–18.00 1 Mar–13 Mar; 09.00–19.00 14 Mar–20 Mar & Oct; 08.00–20.00 21 Mar–Sept ⓦ www.opapisa.it ⓝ Bus: LAM Rossa. Admission charge

Palazzo Reale (Royal Palace)

The former residence of the Medici family (in the 15th century) is of historic rather than aesthetic interest, though there is a rather intriguing collection that once belonged to the influential House of Savoy inside. Lungarno Pacinotti 46 (050) 926 539 09.00–14.30 Mon–Fri, 09.00–13.30 Sat. Bus: LAM Verde; LAM Rossa. Admission charge

RETAIL THERAPY

113 ViaSantaMaria Lose yourself in the choice presented by this shop full of chess sets with pieces representing knights, soldiers, Romans and the four republics. There's also a good selection of ceramics and marble. Via Santa Maria 113B (050) 554 731 www.113viasantamaria.it 10.30–19.00 Thur–Tues Bus: 4, 21

Bottega d'Arte A sort of thrift shop with modern and antique picture framing and art work, furniture and ceramics. Piazza Cavallotti 10 (050) 553 000 09.30–13.00, 16.00–20.00 Mon–Fri, 09.30–13.00 Sat; also open 2nd Sun of month Bus: 4, 21

Hi-Tech Malibu Boutique Designer and good-quality clothing, boots and bags for men and women. There's another branch in Borgo Stretto and one in Viareggio. Via Santa Maria 167 (050) 560 384 09.00–19.30 Bus: 4, 21

Società Cooperative Artieri Alabastro Sells all kinds of handcrafted alabaster figurines from Volterra (see page 116). Perfect for a (extremely fragile) souvenir. ⓐ Via Santa Maria 112 ❶ (050) 561 845 ⓦ www.artierialabastro.it ⓛ 09.30–18.00 ⓝ Bus: 4, 21

Le Toscanacce Dried pasta shop that has big kitsch appeal: there are bags of pasta shaped like the buildings in the Campo dei Miracoli, and coloured pasta representing the Italian flag. ⓐ Via Santa Maria 157 ❶ (050) 830 929 ⓛ 10.00–19.00 ⓝ Bus: 4, 21

TAKING A BREAK

Al Bagno di Nerone £ ❶ Serves good, cheap thin-sliced pizza that's delicious and popular with students. Situated at the corner of Via Cardinale Pietro Maffi. ⓐ Via C Fedeli 23 ❶ (050) 551 085 ⓛ 12.00–15.00, 19.00–00.00 ⓝ Bus: 4

Cibitalia £ ❷ Freshly made sandwiches while you wait. There are plenty of foodie gifts nicely boxed to browse and tables outside with a view of the Leaning Tower. ⓐ Via Cardinale Pietro Maffi 36 ❶ (050) 551 685 ⓛ 10.00–18.00 ⓝ Bus: 4

Panetteria Antiche Tradizioni £ ❸ Bread and cold meat arranged in intriguing ways. The façade is false but interesting. ⓐ Via Santa Maria 66 ❶ Mobile: 347 6752 940 ⓛ 08.00–20.00 ⓝ Bus: 4, 21

Pizzeria Trattoria Toscana £ ❹ Good value for money, efficient and courteous staff and a big choice of pizza. ⓐ Via Santa Maria 163 ❶ (050) 561 876 ⓛ 12.30–15.00, 19.30–23.00 Tues–Sun ⓝ Bus: 4, 21

Roberto Pizzeria Gastronomia £ ❺ Bakes fresh pizza and bread daily. Good range of snacks and drinks, plus wines and food to take home. Via Roma 7 ❶ (050) 293 64 ● 07.30–14.30, 17.00–21.00 Ⓝ Bus: 4, 21

La Foresta ££ ❻ Situated on the Marina di Pisa, this no-frills but big thrills (in the food sense) pizzeria and restaurant is popular with holidaymakers in the summer months. Reservation recommended. ⓐ Via Litoranea 2 ❶ (050) 350 82 ● 12.30–15.00, 19.00–23.00

AFTER DARK

RESTAURANTS

Osteria i Santi £ ❼ Reasonably priced restaurant very near the Leaning Tower that serves excellent Tuscan-style food. It's very busy at lunchtime, so try to go in the evening. Reservation recommended. ⓐ Via Santa Maria 71 ❶ (050) 280 81 ● 12.00–15.00, 19.00–22.00 Ⓝ Bus: 4, 21

The Wall Club ££ ❽ Pizzeria and cocktail bar just a few steps from Campo dei Miracoli. Big screen TV to watch the football and live music and dance nights at the weekends. ⓐ Via Cardinale Pietro Maffi 26 ❶ (050) 830 989 Ⓦ www.thewallclub.com ● 11.00–14.00 Mon, 20.00–00.00 Tues, 11.00–14.00, 20.00–00.00 Wed–Sun Ⓝ Bus: 4, 21

Da Bruno £££ ❾ Out of the doorway of Porta Luca. Well-known top class restaurant with an excellent reputation for fine food. ⓐ Via Luigi Bianchi ❶ (050) 560 818 Ⓦ www.pisaonline.it/trattoriadabruno ● 12.00–15.00, 19.00–22.30 Ⓝ Bus: 4

Osteria dei Mille £££ ⑩ Excellent food, with special applause for the desserts. Nice place to choose for a romantic dinner. ⓐ Via dei Mille 32 ⓘ (050) 556 263 ⓛ 20.00–23.00 Tues–Sun ⓝ Bus: 4

BARS & CLUBS

Miracles Cocktail and wine bar that's popular with students – always a good sign. ⓐ Via Padre Agostino da Montefeltro, Marina di Pisa ⓘ Mobile: 338 2769 285 ⓛ 19.30–02.00 Tues–Thur, 19.30–21.00 Sun ⓝ Bus: CPT Line 010

Pappafico A hip crowd flocks here every weekend and there are special 70s, 80s and 90s nights in summer. ⓐ Via Litoranea 14, Marina di Pisa ⓘ (050) 350 35 ⓦ www.ilpappafico.it ⓛ 22.00–04.00 Fri & Sat ⓝ Bus: CPT Line 010

● Pappafico draws clubbers to the seaside every weekend

Centre of Town & San Francesco Quarter

This area covers the central and Eastern parts of Pisa, including the historic centre. These districts are quieter than that of Campo dei Miracoli, and really repay investigation. Once again, the most pleasurable way to get around is on foot.

SIGHTS & ATTRACTIONS

Arsenale

In 1998, during construction planning for a new railway station, builders discovered underground 16 perfectly preserved ancient ships dating from the first century BC to the fourth century AD, just a few yards away from the Campo dei Miracoli. Even their cargoes were intact, and other finds include the complete skeletons of a sailor and his dog. The Arsenale is opposite the Chiesa San Paolo a Ripa d'Arno and, although plans remain sketchy, it is hoped that this will be the site for a museum that will be built around these magnificent specimens. For now, archaeologists are still feverishly buzzing around a site that is telling them a great deal about life in Etruscan and Roman Pisa. ☎ (050) 512 1919 ⏱ Tours: 10.00, 11.00, 12.00, 14.30, 15.30 Fri & Sat; other times by appointment 🚍 Bus: 6, 21

Chiesa di San Francesco

This church once held the private chapels of noble Pisan families, and it was constructed to a remarkably modest design to reflect the relatively ascetic views of St Francis. The interior contains a charming restored fresco that tells the story of the Virgin

○ Chiesa di San Stefano dei Cavalieri, the only Renaissance church in Pisa

Osteria dei Cavalieri

Osteria I Santi 274

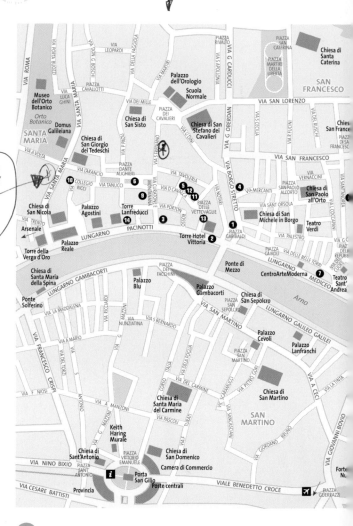

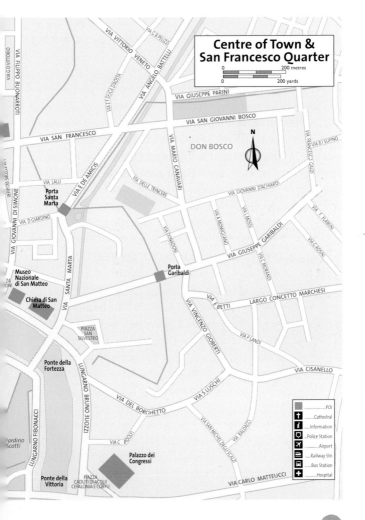

Mary. If you want to visit, you should call in advance to make an appointment. ⓐ Piazza di San Francesco ⓣ (050) 544 091 ⓝ Bus: 4

Chiesa San Michele in Borgo

This 11th-century church demonstrates some intriguing architectural juxtapositions. For example, its Romanesque ledges are decorated with arches and heads carved to a clearly Gothic design. The interior is a treasure trove. There's a marble crucifix by Nino Pisano and an old crypt that's believed to predate this structure. You can also see some 17th-century political graffiti on the walls in the form of a propagandist inscription lavishly praising students who were up for election to the post of University Chancellor.

PALAZZO DELL'OROLOGIO (CLOCK TOWER)

An impressive piece of architecture set in the Piazza dei Cavalieri. In early medieval times this square was the headquarters of local politicians, but it later became the seat of the Knights Templar, a sort of religious elite military squad that was formed to protect pilgrims and soldiers returning from the Crusades and that ended up being, for 200 years, the crack military unit of its time. Today it is owned by the University of Pisa and is used for academic purposes, including accommodating the library for the Scuola Normale (see opposite). Although the palace is not open for visiting, one glimpse at its exterior will transport you to a world of daring deeds and subterfuge. ⓐ Piazza dei Cavalieri ⓝ Bus: 4

ⓐ Borgo Stretto ⓛ 08.00–11.00, 15.00–17.00 Ⓝ Bus: 4

Chiesa di San Paolo all'Orto

Definitely one for the archaeologists: a permanent exhibition of restored chalk statues from Roman and Greek mythology is on display, with explanations on restoration work by the Faculty of Architecture and Science of Pisa University. ⓐ Piazza San Paolo all'Orto ⓣ Mobile: 346 3236 607 Ⓦ www.arch.unipi.it ⓛ 08.30–13.30, 14.00–17.00 Wed Ⓝ Bus: 4

Chiesa di San Stefano dei Cavalieri

This is of interest on two counts: it is the only Renaissance church in Pisa, and its superb interior is richly decorated with scenes from past battles of the Knights of St Stephen. This was an order set up in the late 16th century by Cosimo I de Medici to patrol the Mediterranean and combat Ottoman pirates. The sumptuous booty from their clashes adorns the church, which also contains a beautiful wooden ceiling and some excellent paintings. In all then, a lovely church and a magnificent gallery. ⓐ Piazza dei Cavalieri ⓛ 10.00–19.00 Mon–Sat, 13.00–19.30 Sun Ⓝ Bus: 4. Admission charge

Scuola Normale

Despite its name, there's nothing normal about this university, which was originally set up by Napoleon in 1811 as an outpost of l'École normale supérieure de Paris. This is the institution that really underlined Pisa's reputation as a centre of excellence. A sort of Oxbridge and then some, only the very brightest students are admitted. Visitors are not allowed in, lest they rend the academic

◔ Scuola Normale, Pisa's centre of academic excellence

vibe asunder but the façade is beautiful and well worth a snap.
🅰 Piazza dei Cavalieri 🅦 www.sns.it 🅝 Bus: 4

CULTURE

CentroArteModerna

Almost coming as a relief among all the churches, here's an
art gallery with collections and exhibitions of some of the best
modern art in Tuscany. 🅐 Lungarno Mediceo 26 🅣 (050) 542 630
🅦 www.centroartemoderna.com 🅛 10.00–12.30, 16.30–19.30
Mon–Sat, 17.00–19.30 Sun 🅝 Bus: LAM Verde

Museo Nazionale di San Matteo

A must for art-lovers, this riverside museum leads visitors through
a splendidly illustrated history of Pisan and Florentine art. Its theme,
from which it strays quite gloriously at times, is religious work, and
there are some wonderful pieces by local geniuses, Nicola and
Giovanni Pisano (see page 97). There is also a fine collection of
medieval paintings on wood panelling. 🅐 Lungarno Mediceo
🅣 (050) 541 865 🅛 08.30–19.00 Mon–Fri, 09.00–13.30 Sat & Sun
🅝 Bus: 4. Admission charge

Teatro Sant'Andrea

This church, which has its origins as a Roman temple, was
taken over by a student theatre foundation in 1986. Now,
although the combination of the words 'student' and 'theatre'
strikes terror into the heart of most people, this theatre certainly
merits its reputation as a breeding ground for talented practitioners
of drama and dance. 🅐 Via del Cuore (near the Tribunale)

☏ (050) 542 364 ⓦ www.teatrosantandrea.it ⏰ Opening times depend on the production Ⓝ Bus: 4

Teatro Verdi

Certainly the city's leading performing arts centre, the Teatro is a modern temple to showbiz, whether it's in the form of opera, whose season runs from September to March, or drama (of all kinds) and dance, which run from November to May. ⓐ Via Palestro 40 ☏ (050) 941 111 ⓦ www.teatrodipisa.pi.it ⏰ Opening times depend on the production; box office: 16.00–19.00 Tue & Thurs, 11.00–13.00, 16.00–19.00 Wed, Fri & Sat Ⓝ Bus: 4

RETAIL THERAPY

L'Arcolaio Bijoux Jewellery Some unique jewellery and accessories are on display for sale in this very pretty little shop on the corner near the fruit market. ⓐ Via Curtatone e Montanara 30 ☏ (050) 573 955 ⏰ 10.00–13.30, 14.00–20.00 Ⓝ Bus: 4

La Botteghina della Passerella The huge variety of ornamental objects, household items, ceramics, boxed statuettes, glassware and silver on show here make this the sort of place that you enter in search of presents for the folks back home and exit with lots of presents for yourself. ⓐ Lungarno Gambacorti 42 ☏ (050) 485 72 ⓦ www.paginegialle.it/botteghinadellapasserella ⏰ 09.00–13.00, 15.30–19.30 Mon–Sat Ⓝ Bus: 4

Gabrio Staff A hair stylist, make-up artiste and master of the manicure to whom a visit is strongly recommended as an

DE BONDT CHOCOLATES

This shop is something special, not least because it has been acclaimed as being one of the ten best chocolatiers in the world. Paul De Bondt, a Dutch confectioner, and Cecilia Iacobelli, a local designer, run this chocolate shop whose products showcase the former's artistry and the latter's flair. You simply won't find superior handmade chocolates anywhere in Italy and be warned: even those who claim not to have a sweet tooth in their head emerge from De Bondt as chronic chocoholics. What's more, De Bondt also has a workshop in Visignamo, a few kilometres from Pisa, where guided tours allow visitors to see the chocolate-making process and enjoy tastings afterwards. There are also training courses available on advanced techniques of chocolate production, so this could be a great idea for a holiday combined with some learning. ⓐ Lungarno Pacinotti 5 ⓣ (050) 316 0073 ⓛ 09.30–20.00 Mon–Sat (also 16.00–20.00 second Sun of month) ⓦ www.debondt.it ⓝ Bus: 4

experience, for the shop's motto is: 'We want demanding, insistent, nasty and provocative customers'. Go for it. ⓐ Via Mercanti 9 ⓣ (050) 542 374 ⓛ 08.30–19.30 Mon–Sat ⓝ Bus: 4

Libreria Ghibellina A very pleasant bookstore with a massive stock that includes many an English-language volume. ⓐ Borgo Stretto 37 ⓣ (050) 580 277 ⓛ 09.30–20.00 (until later July & Aug) ⓝ Bus: 4

Max il Cuoiaio Leather goods sold and repaired. There's that incredible smell of fresh leather as you enter the shop and some very stylish bags on sale. ⓐ Via D Cavalca 57 ⓣ (050) 574 299 ⓦ www.maxilcuoiaio.it ⓛ 09.00–13.00, 15.30–20.00 Mon–Sat

Nato Libero Big-name sports clothing and brands including Murphy & Nye, Marlboro Classic, Hilfiger. ⓐ Borgo Stretto 36 ⓣ (050) 971 1404 ⓛ 09.00–13.00, 15.00–19.30 Ⓝ Bus: 4

Nine T Nine Cent Paradise Although this quirky shop is a place where everything costs 99 cents, it's in a completely different league from the sturdy British Pound shop and is just the place to pop into for the practical items you always forget to pack or run out of too soon. What's more, this is just the place to pack up a kitsch gift for your post-modernist chums (who'll never know how little it cost). ⓐ Via G Carducci 77 ⓣ Mobile: 328 9635 180 ⓦ www.cent-shop.com ⓛ 09.30–20.00 Ⓝ Bus: 4

Royale Denim A vintage and fashion store for men and women that turns up many an item of real Italian flair. ⓐ Piazza San Paolo all'Orto 2 ⓣ (050) 721 0558 ⓛ 09.00–13.30, 15.00–19.30 ⓦ www.royale-store.it Ⓝ Bus: 4

Sivieri Perfumes Just the place for something a little different for dabbing behind your earlobes. There are plenty of ideas for gifts to take home, including boxed sets of body products, cosmetics and perfumes. ⓐ Via Borgo Stretto 33 ⓣ (050) 580 880 ⓛ 09.00–13.00, 15.00–19.00 Mon–Sat Ⓝ Bus: 4

Valenti Top-class clothes and shoes by well-known designers, including Prada, Gucci, Fendi, Moncler and Dolce & Gabbana. You'll pick up some real bargains here, including items that you won't find outside Italy. ⓐ Borgo Stretto 28 ⓣ (050) 580 139 ⓛ 09.00–13.00, 15.00–19.30 ⓝ Bus: 4

TAKING A BREAK

La Bottega del Gelato £ ❶ Locally renowned for serving strange but deliciously flavoured ice cream. Highly recommended among an array of oddities that would leave Heston Blumenthal feeling distinctly weirded out is the liquorice and cookie ice cream. ⓐ Piazza Garibaldi 11 ⓣ (050) 575 467 ⓛ 11.00–22.00 ⓝ Bus: 4

Caffè dell'Ussero £ ❷ Famous coffee house that opened in 1775 in what remains a beautiful red-brick building. A number of famous guests have passed through its doors, including John Ruskin in 1840, but it doesn't rest on its laurels: it still serves up a mean coffee and is a vibrant meeting place and fabulous spot for some people-watching. ⓐ Lungarno Pacinotti 27 ⓣ (050) 581 100 ⓦ www.ussero.com ⓛ 10.00–20.00 Mon–Sat ⓝ Bus: 4

Gelateria Naturale de Coltelli £ ❸ Using only natural ingredients and fresh fruits such as mangoes, oranges and figs, this gorgeous parlour makes traditional and flavoured ice cream without preservatives or added colourings. ⓐ Lungarno Pacinotti 23 ⓣ (050) 541 611 ⓦ www.decoltelli.com ⓛ 11.00–23.30 Mon–Thur, 11.00–00.30 Fri & Sat ⓝ Bus: 4

Lo Sfizio £ **④** Primarily recommended for its structural beauty, this café has a wonderfully restored façade with arched curtained windows. A truly elegant place to stop for tea. **ⓐ** Borgo Stretto 54 **ⓘ** (050) 580 281 **ⓛ** 07.00–01.00 **ⓝ** Bus: 4

Pisa Pasta £ **⑤** Here you'll experience an intriguing phenomenon: quick snack pasta from machines. Simply insert the coins and out pops your pasta. There are also drinks and dessert machines.

● *Elegant Lo Sfizio in Borgo Stretto*

It might be handy if you are in a hurry and is great for a giggle, but there's no guarantee that the pasta is like Mamma claims she used to make. ⓐ Via D Cavalca 80 ⓑ 09.00–01.00 ⓝ Bus: 4

Caffetteria Dantesca di Ceragioli Matteo ££ ⓺ Expect a typical Tuscan menu that includes such delights as *Ragù di carne alla fiorentina* (a wondrous Florentine meat sauce) and a beautiful mural of Dante's *Inferno* inside. Soup is a specialty and there's a good-value lunch menu that you can enjoy at tables in the square outside. ⓐ Piazza Dante Alighieri 8 ⓣ (050) 462 80 ⓑ 08.00–00.00 ⓦ www.caffetteriadantesca.it ⓝ Bus: 4

AFTER DARK

RESTAURANTS
Babette Food and Art Café £ ⓻ An intriguing modern eaterie that offers exhibitions, cooking demonstrations, theatre productions and live music while you munch your way through dainty versions of Italian classics. ⓐ Lungarno Mediceo 15 ⓣ (050) 991 3302 ⓦ www.babettepisa.it ⓑ 17.00–02.00 Tues–Sun ⓝ Bus: 4

Il Colonnino Osteria Enoteca ££ ⓼ In the act of restoring this old wine cellar, the owner found a small Etruscan column which is now on display in a corner of the restaurant. This is one of the places that's registered to serve *mucca pisana* meat (see page 29) and you'll be seduced by the delicious starters. ⓐ Via Sant'Andrea 37 ⓣ (050) 313 8430 ⓦ www.ilcolonnino.it ⓑ 12.30–14.00, 19.00–22.00 Tues–Sun ⓝ Bus: 4

Osteria del Porton Rosso ££ ⑨ Perfect for a relaxing dinner, this insouciant osteria serves a must-sample cheese-and-pear dessert. ⓐ Vicolo del Porton Rosso ⓣ (050) 580 566 ⓦ www.osteriadelportonrosso.com ⓛ 11.00–15.00, 19.30–00.00 Mon–Sat ⓝ Bus : 4

Vecchio Teatro Restaurant ££ ⑩ Great value set menu with typical Pisan food. The real USP is the academic opportunity: the cook likes to present and talk about the food he serves. He'll tell you about Pisa's history, too, and he's a massively charismatic lecturer. ⓐ Via Collegio Ricci 2 ⓣ (050) 202 10 ⓛ 12.00–15.00, 19.30–23.30 ⓝ Bus: 4

Il Campano £££ ⑪ Squashed in between two huge buildings, this little tower house restaurant serves Tuscan cuisine that's uniformly excellent but that really stands out on the antipasti. There is seating upstairs, too, and reservations are definitely recommended. ⓐ Via D Cavalca 19 ⓣ (050) 580 585 ⓛ 19.30–22.45 Thur, 12.30–15.00, 19.30–22.45 Fri–Tues ⓝ Bus: 4

Osteria La Mescita £££ ⑫ Good selection of fish and one of the few places you'll get bona fide *mucca pisana* meat dishes. On top of that, it's a nice place for a romantic evening. ⓐ Via D Cavalca 2 ⓣ (050) 957 019 ⓛ 12.30–14.30, 19.45–23.00 Tues–Sat ⓝ Bus: 4

Ristoro delle Vettovaglie £££ ⑬ Stylish and well-known restaurant that combines Italian brio with Tuscan warmth. ⓐ Piazza delle Vettovaglie 33 ⓣ (050) 574 024

Ⓦ www.caffetteriadellevettovaglie.com Ⓛ 19.00–01.00
Mon–Thur, 19.00–02.00 Fri & Sat Ⓝ Bus : 4

Il Vecchio Dado £££ Ⓝ An exclusive address that's perfect
for a romantic dinner, with an inspiring fresh fish menu and
succulent meat dishes. Reservations are strongly recommended
at weekends. Ⓐ Lungarno Pacinotti 21-22 Ⓣ (050) 580 900
Ⓛ 12.30–14.30, 19.00–22.30 Ⓝ Bus: 4

BARS & CLUBS
Bazeel Music Pub and Argentine Bar Hip, young and trendy crowd
every evening with tables outside in the square. A popular meeting
place for students. That means: fun. Ⓐ Piazza Garibaldi Ⓣ Mobile:
349 1902 586 Ⓦ www.bazeel.it Ⓛ 18.00–02.00 Ⓝ Bus: 4

Borderline Club Heavy rock club with such treats as special tribute
nights to Jimi Hendrix and Queen. It occasionally strays into live
reggae, jazz and blues. Ⓐ Via Vernaccini 7 Ⓣ (050) 580 577
Ⓛ 23.00–04.00 Ⓝ Bus: 4

Sweet & Sour 70s Pub Serves good cocktails and has a nice
selection of other drinks. It's a disco kind of place with a young,
vivacious crowd. Ⓐ Lungarno Mediceo 52 Ⓣ Mobile: 333 3719 121
Ⓦ www.sweetandsour.it Ⓛ 18.00–02.00 Ⓝ Bus: 4

Temple Bar Small Irish pub in the square that attracts British
tourists with its selection of beer and spirits. Ⓐ Piazza Cairoli 10
Ⓣ (050) 830 989 Ⓛ 11.00–23.00 Ⓝ Bus: 4

Over the bridges

Even in a city that's full of beautiful architecture, this south-of-the-river area still stands out with its richness of churches and *palazzi*. This is really a daytime part of the city, encompassing as it does busy Lungarno Gambacorti and Lungarno Galileo Galilei and the popular shopping street of Corso Italia. Buses run all over the area, but it was, like the rest of the city, really made to be explored on foot.

SIGHTS & ATTRACTIONS

Chiesa di San Domenico

This modest church, which has, compared with the other ecclesiastical buildings in the area, a distinctly coy charm, boasts a delightful provenance: it was built for the daughter of the city's 14th-century ruler Pietro Gambacorti, and evolved into a convent. Its interior décor is modest; its treasures few; its atmosphere is stunning. San Domenico is open during mass only, the irregularity of which makes it prudent to pop in and arrange your visit in advance. Even if you only go in order to take a breather in between bouts of shopping, do go. ⓐ Corso Italia Ⓝ Bus: LAM Verde; LAM Rossa

Chiesa di San Martino

Far less reticent a church than San Domenico, San Martino sets out its stall con brio. Architecture buffs will spot features that span the roughly 500 years it took to build (between 1062 and 1610), and art fans will love the paintings that make this church

◉ *Detail of mosaic inlay from the Palazzo Gambacorti*

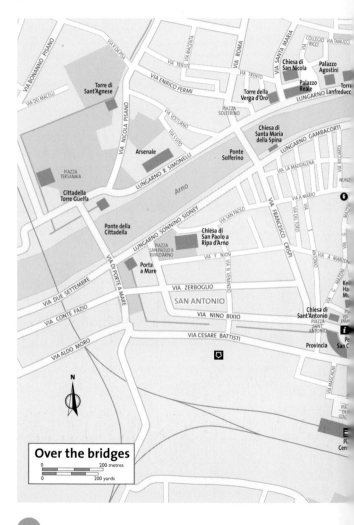

Over the bridges

0 — 200 metres

0 — 200 yards

6 Sfizo   babette FoodcArt

OVER THE BRIDGES

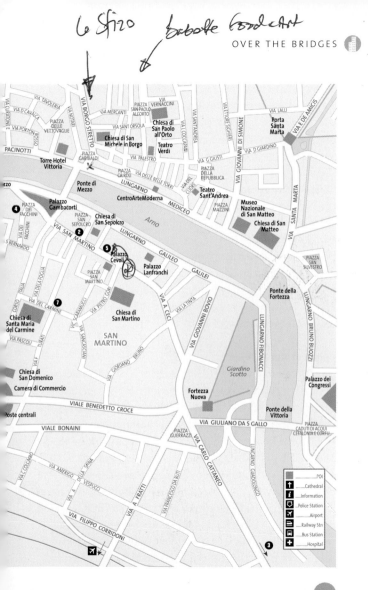

an ecclesiastical gallery. The portal features an exquisite copy of a marble carving by Andrea Pisano that depicts St Martin and the poor. Again, the fact that this church admits visitors only during mass renders making arrangements in advance very wise. ⓐ Piazza San Martino ① (050) 495 68 ⓝ Bus: LAM Verde; LAM Rossa

Chiesa di San Paolo a Ripa d'Arno

You'll soon spot that this church's architecture – which was set in place in around 930 – is similar to that of the Duomo on Campo dei Miracoli (see page 66), both being prime examples of Pisan Romanesque, a highly influential medieval style that's typified by beautifully ornate façades. The inside's not bad, either, particularly the romantic octagonal chapel of St Agatha. Phone in advance if you would like to visit. ⓐ Lungarno Sonnino Sidney ① (050) 415 15 ⓝ Bus: 6

Chiesa di San Sepolcro

No small air of mystery is conjured by this church, which was designed by Diotisalvi – he of the Baptistery (see page 58) – for those courters of controversy, the Knights Templar. Its octagonal shape echoes that of the Holy Sepulchre church in Jerusalem, whence the Knights had lifted some highly significant relics. They ended up in storage here. It is said that the well by the vestry contains water with miraculous powers. Despite these distinctly Da Vinci Codeian resonances, the church was actually constructed in the 12th century as a highly practical one-stop reintegration-into-normal-life shop for soldiers and their retinues as they returned from the Crusades. ⓐ Piazza San Sepolcro ① (050) 233 55 ⓛ 09.00–12.00 ⓝ Bus: LAM Verde

Chiesa di Santa Maria della Spina

This fabulously Gothic church (its façade is a master class in Gothic ornamentation) has a moving history: in 1871, it was moved brick-by-brick to save it from being ruined by the river and now stands rather incongruously on the pavement just off the Ponte Solferino bridge. It was built in 1230 to protect what was alleged to be a thorn (*spina*) from Christ's crucifixion crown; the thorn is in the Church of Santa Chiara (see page 64). ⓐ Lungarno Gambacorti ⓛ 10.00–14.00 Tues–Thur, 10.00–14.00, 15.00–17.00 Fri & Sat. Admission charge ⓥ Bus: 6

⬥ *Chiesa di Santa Maria della Spina is right on the edge of the Arno river*

Giardino Scotto & Fortezza Nuova

A wall goes around these pretty gardens, and there's a walkway above with arches that has a view of the river. This was once part of Pisa's defensive wall which was heavily bombarded over the years. The fort was built after the wall. Recently, floating pontoons and a small bridge have been added to give better public access. During the summer months an open air cinema and occasional exhibitions take place. ⓐ Lungarno Fibonacci ⓛ 09.30–16.30 Nov–Jan; 09.00–18.00 Feb, Mar & Oct; 09.00–20.00 Apr–June & Sept; 08.00–20.00 July & Aug ⓝ Bus: LAM Verde

Palazzo Cevoli

There's a touch of 16th-century romance behind the story of this fabulous palace's construction. Prince Fredrick IV of Denmark fell in love with local stunner, Maddelena Trenta, but they couldn't marry as he was a Protestant and she was a Catholic. Clearly something of a faint-heart, Frederick decided to concentrate on his career and went back to Denmark to become King. Maddelena joined a convent and became a nun... but their love refused to die and Frederick kept coming back for some dodgy visits. This was his *pied à terre* while he was in town. Sadly, the palace is not open to the public, but its frescoed exterior can still be admired. ⓐ Via San Martino 108 ⓝ Bus: LAM Verde

Porta San Gilio

The building work for an underground car park has now become an excavation site, as remains of an Etruscan village have been found. Details of the excavation are set up on boards around the square. At the moment there's no access to the public but a proposed

idea to allow viewing of the site in future is being considered.
ⓐ Piazza Vittorio Emanuele Ⓝ Bus: LAM Verde

CULTURE

Palazzo Blu

In November 2008, this bright blue palace reopened after massive
renovations, having been re-themed as a 4,000 sq metre (4,374 sq
yard) 'palace of art and culture'. Visitors can expect exhibitions
and cutting edge shows quite at odds with the lavishly decorated
interior of this one-time residence of Count Giuli. ⓐ Lungarno
Gambacorti ❶ (050) 500 197 ⓦ www.palazzoblu.it 🕒 16.00–19.00
Tues–Fri, 11.00–13.00 Sat & Sun ❶ Sat & Sun guided tours
16.00–19.00 Ⓝ Bus: LAM Verde. Admission charge

> **PISA'S SPECTACULAR SCULPTURAL SUPERSTARS**
> Although linguists will realise why the surname Pisano
> is not rare in these parts, its two most eminent bearers,
> the father and son team Nicola (c1220–c1284) and
> Giovanni (c1250–c1314), made it their own by virtue of
> being monumental architectural and sculptural superstars.
> Nicola could be said to be the Elvis of sculpture in the way
> that he took regional styles and mixed them to create
> something new, and thus set the world alight. He is
> recognised as having melded together Christian and
> European styles and then, on top of that, he mixed Gothic
> and Romanesque. This is the sculptural equivalent of

mixing rap with punk and then throwing in some jazz-funk and ragga to produce something new and wonderful. When he took over work on the Battistero (see page 58) from Diotisalvi, people expected that he would do a workmanlike job, and stick to the original plans. He did exactly the opposite, doing a virtuoso job and tearing up the plans completely. It was in the Battistero that he revealed his remarkable presentation of human faces, even the smallest of which display subtle human emotions. Nicola's work made Pisa the focal point of European sculpture.

Although Giovanni could not hope to emulate the splash made by his father, he carried on his work by injecting ever more Gothic – which means ever more drama – into Nicola's style. Making his base in Pisa in the 1290s, he worked all over Tuscany, and probably the best extant example of his work is the Madonna that resides in the Chiesa di Santa Maria della Spina (see page 95). Also in Pisa is his boldest statement of intent, his polygonal pulpit for the Duomo.

Palazzo Gambacorti

Now the town hall, this building was once owned by the powerful Gambacorti family. The palace has Gothic windows on the upper floor, and civil marriages take place in the Hall of the Coat of Arms. The frescoed walls and ceilings depict past battles in Pisa. Pietro Gambacorti, Lord of Pisa, was murdered here in 1393 by conspirators. In the Red Hall that used to be the

Mayor's Office, the walls are covered in red wallpaper and there's a fresco by the Melani brothers that shows Pisa paying homage to San Ranieri. In collaboration with the department of Languages and Literature of the University of Pisa there are guided tours to see the three main rooms of interest. There's a maximum of 20 people allowed to visit so you need to book a place. ⓐ Lungarno Gambacorti ⓣ (050) 910 350 ⓔ tourist-point@comunepisa.it ⓝ Bus: 4

RETAIL THERAPY

L'Artista del Vetro This workshop uses procedures for glass-making taken from documents from medieval times to create stained glass panel doors, decorative mirrors and lampshades. Even if you don't buy anything, you can regard L'Arista as a gallery of the glass-maker's art. Careful how you sashay among the aisles! ⓐ Via Carlo Cattaneo 129 ⓣ (050) 500 0078 ⓛ 09.30–12.00, 15.30–17.00 ⓝ Bus: 8

Bacchus Wine Specialists A vast assortment of wine from Tuscany, including gift-boxed bottles to take home, and particularly friendly staff. ⓐ Via Mascagni 1 ⓣ (050) 500 560 ⓦ www.bacchusenoteca.com ⓛ 09.00–19.00 ⓝ Bus: LAM Verde

Batini If you fancy some unique bling, this family-run jewellery store sells decorative silverware and has a large selection of gold and silver necklaces, bracelets and rings. ⓐ Corso Italia ⓣ (050) 503 977 ⓛ 09.30–13.00, 16.00–20.00 ⓝ Bus: LAM Verde

Ego Boutique Ego purveys the latest in women's fashion. It's a little expensive, but the quality is excellent. Should you be assailed by the urge to give into temptation, there is no finer place in which to spend next month's Christmas club money on some wicked threads. @ Lungarno Gambacorti 25 ☎ (050) 220 1471 ⓦ www.egoconceptstore.com ⏰ 09.00–19.30 Mon–Sat Ⓝ Bus: 4

Profumerie Douglas Worth nipping into for the fragrance alone, this shop sells a wide range of perfumes, soaps, creams and cosmetics, gift boxed items to take home and special offers that change every week. @ Corso Italia 123 ☎ (050) 220 0201 ⏰ 09.00–19.00 Ⓝ Bus: LAM Verde

Samarcanda Handcrafted leather shoes for ladies of all ages. @ Via Oberdan 26, off Borgo Stretto ☎ (050) 542 441 ⏰ 09.30–13.00, 15.30–20.00 Mon–Sat Ⓝ Bus: LAM Verde

TAKING A BREAK

Il Pomo d'Oro Pizzeria £ ❶ Offers door-to-door delivery, take away and eat in service. You can get slabs of delicious pizza for €5, snacks and pasta dishes in this simple diner that's perfect when you want to fill your (handcrafted leather) boots without spending too much. @ Via Nunziatina 13 ☎ (050) 500 015 ⏰ 12.00–14.30, 18.30–23.30 Wed–Mon Ⓝ Bus: LAM Verde

Ristorante Numero 11 £ ❷ Service is non-existent here: you go to the bar, order your food from a variety of classic Italian choices and take it to your long table. It's a place where you can eat something fast and then go. A real bonus is that there are plenty of vegetarian dishes. ⓐ Via San Martino 47 ⓣ (050) 272 82 ⓦ www.numeroundici.it ⓛ 12.00–22.00 Mon–Sat ⓝ Bus: LAM Verde

Trattoria Pizzeria Sapori Toscani £ ❸ You can build up an appetite by walking along the river Piagge to this pizzeria in the village of Riglione. It's got a warm and friendly atmosphere and you can eat in, take away or call for delivery. ⓐ Via Fiorentina 461 ⓣ (050) 980 135 ⓛ 12.00–15.00, 19.00–22.00 ⓝ Bus: LAM Verde

AFTER DARK

RESTAURANTS

Bagus Wine & Food ££ ❹ 'Bagus' is an Indonesian word meaning 'all is well', and it certainly is here. Their logo is the cockerel, which is the symbol of excellence used by the Tuscan Knights. The quality of the wide range of Italian classics available here makes that logo appropriate. ⓐ Piazza dei Facchini 13 ⓣ (050) 261 96 ⓦ www.bagusristorante.it ⓛ 12.00–15.00, 19.00–22.00 Mon–Fri, 19.00–22.00 Sat ⓝ Bus: LAM Verde

Ristorante Enoteca L'Etichetta ££ ❺ A notably pretty restaurant with a varied Tuscan menu that offers such treats as *panzanella* (a simple – but simply glorious – salad with fresh tomatoes, onions and basil). ⓐ Via San Martino 89 ⓣ (050) 240 80 ⓛ 12.30–15.00, 19.00–22.30 Mon–Sat, 13.00–15.00 Sun ⓝ Bus: LAM Verde

Hostaria Pizzeria Le Repubbliche Marinare £££ ❻ The speciality here is the so-called 'pizza of the four republics', which gives you four sumptuous different slices. The desserts are scrumptious and artistically presented. ⓐ Vicolo del Ricciardi 8, Via G Mazzini ⓘ (050) 205 06 ⓛ 17.00–23.00 Tues–Sun ⓝ Bus: LAM Verdi

Osteria Il Capodaglio £££ ❼ Basic pizzas and pastas, but bear in mind that 'basic' in this part of the world is a synonym for 'delicious'. It has smoking and no smoking rooms and a large selection of Tuscan wine. ⓐ Via del Carmine 34 ⓘ (050) 200 38 ⓦ www.ilcapodaglio.it ⓛ 12.00–15.30, 20.00–23.30 Mon–Sat (closed Thur in winter) ⓝ Bus: LAM Verde

PUBS & BARS
Lo Spaventapasseri Pub 'The Scarecrow Pub' has tavern food to take away or eat in and a lively atmosphere that never strays into the raucous. For those missing the pubs back home, there's a dart board and a humongous TV. ⓐ Via dei Facchini 3 ⓘ (050) 440 67 ⓛ 19.00–00.45 Tues–Sun ⓝ Bus: LAM Verde

Mimi Café A spectacular medieval wine cellar that retains its original walls and has been elegantly restored as a wine bar. Great for an aperitif before dinner. ⓐ Via G Mazzini 70 ⓘ Mobile: 333 8400 9427 ⓛ 19.00–01.00 Mon–Thur, 19.00–02.00 Fri & Sat ⓝ Bus: LAM Verde

ⓓ *Volterra, a cornucopia of architectural beauty*

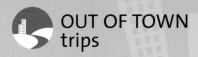

Monte Pisano

There are many small villages of immense historical interest clustered on and around the rural and highly forested Monte Pisano. What follows is merely a selection of highlights from a truly magnificent part of Tuscany. Sometimes we have listed actual villages as sights or attractions, and at other times we have listed the places in those villages. That is because of the nature of the area: we are dealing with sometimes tiny conurbations that flow into one another without clearly defined limits.

GETTING THERE

To visit the pretty villages in and around Monte Pisano, it's best to go by car following the well signposted SS roads. Otherwise, a short bus or train journey from Pisa's central stations (see pages 48 & 49) will take you along the hills of Monte Pisano.

SIGHTS & ATTRACTIONS

Calci

Steeped in groves, this achingly pretty village is known for the production of olive oil. Situated on the slopes of Monte Pisano, its main feature is the enormous Charterhouse complex, which is divided into a Natural History Museum and a Charterhouse. The former, **Museo di Storia Naturale e del Territorio** (ⓐ Via Roma 79, Certosa di Calci ⓣ (050) 221 2970), is the sort of place that you never imagine stumbling upon in the middle of the countryside;

⬤ *The dreamlike Tuscan landscape*

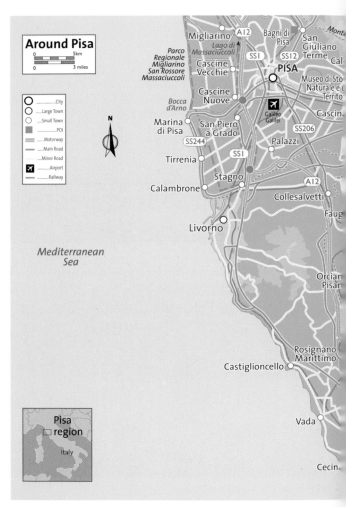

you feel it should be a star attraction in a city. It features hundreds of zoological, mineral and fossil examples, and the University of Pisa is enlarging the museum to include rooms with sound effects from the depths of the sea, life-sized dinosaurs and mythological creatures, an aquarium, a marine skeleton display and an educational room for school groups.

Consorzio La Strada del Vino Costa degli Etruschi

Take this trail to visit vineyards and sample the range of wines from the Tuscan valley. The trail, which you should arrange by phoning the organisers a week or two in advance, is tailored to your wishes and can take place around Monte Pisano and other areas – you choose! ⓐ San Guido 45, Bolgheri ⓣ (0565) 749 768 ⓦ www.lastradadelvino.com

Lari

Lari is situated at the top of three Pisan hills some 25 km (15 miles) southeast of Pisa. Charmingly, you enter the village through an arch that once had a drawbridge, beyond which is a mass of historic delights. Probably its main – and certainly its dominant – feature is the huge castle, **Il Castello dei Vicari** (ⓣ (0587) 687 116 ⓦ www.castellodilari.it), which dates back to 962 and would not be out place in a Vincent Price film. Here you can see the prison, the dungeon known as 'hell', the magistrates' room and the torture room. In the middle of the courtyard there's a chapel with ten cells that allowed the accused (but not the convicted) to attend religious ceremonies. Slightly ironically, perhaps, today the castle is used for weddings. One of Lari's other great attractions is the **Pastificio Tradizionale**

Famiglia Martelli (ⓐ Via San Martino 3, Lari ⓣ (0587) 684 238 ⓦ www.martelli.info). This family-run pasta producing factory introduces you to the secrets of how it is made, and you can also buy the self-same pasta that you've seen being concocted during your visit.

San Giuliano Terme

This is a natural spa resort with thermal waters containing calcium magnesium sulphate that reach a surface temperature of 38°C (100°F). You know what that means? That it's ideal for arthritis, respiratory and cardiovascular problems. San Giuliano Terme also offers beauty treatments, relaxation therapy and top-class hotel facilities: nestling sumptuously within its confines is **Bagni di Pisa** (ⓐ Largo Shelley 18, San Giuliano Terme ⓣ (050) 885 01 ⓦ www.bagnidipisa.com), an 18th-century mansion that is the former residence of the Grand Duke of Lorraine. It is now a spa, but the luxurious atmosphere that drips down its every tile evokes the fact that this building was once frequented by aristocracy from around the world. However, its purpose is not to make you swoon through its ambiance but to offer a restorative experience, and it certainly does that, with its healing thermal water therapies. The spa also offers an impressive menu of beauty treatments and a selection of different massage techniques that are suitable either for a day visit or for a longer stay. The hotel and restaurant offer much in the way of high-end luxury.

The town itself dates back to the Stone Age and is famous for olive oil production and agriculture. To get here, take the SS12 road from Pisa.

Vicopisano

Just 18 km (11 miles) from Pisa town centre, this village is easily accessible by car on the SS67, in the direction of Pontedera. The little settlement dotted with towers makes a nice quiet change from the hustle and bustle of some of the tourist sites. It takes most of the afternoon to see all the towers (see below for a suggested plan of attack) and you will find Vicopisano a most refreshing experience: wherever you look little alleyways lead you to stone-walled medieval houses. A Romanesque church completes the beauty of this unspoiled village.

VICOPISANO TOWER TOUR

So as not to be overwhelmed by the multiple experiences offered here, your first move should be to walk up to the Rocca dei Brunelleschi, a fortress that was completed in 1435 with very high walls and a complex defence system that was designed to make best use of the artillery that was just coming into use at the time. Incidentally, Vicopisano's towers have no addresses, so following them in the order in which we deal with them here is the best and most logical way to enjoy them. Continue down to the Torre del Soccorso, which was actually part of the Fortress; this tower and the surrounding wall allowed soldiers to barricade themselves in during battle. The next structure, Palazzo Pretorio, was the castle-complex prison. Next to that is Palazzo della Vecchia Posta, which is one of the oldest examples of

● *Vicopisano's landscape is dotted with towers*

a medieval palace in the region. Nearby is the Torre di Pietraia, a small tower with a timber balcony. Torre Malanima demonstrates a mixture of building techniques: its oldest parts are made from terracotta. Next, Torre dell'Orologio, the clock tower, is the most interesting and perhaps the most beautiful of the towers. Torri Gemelle (Twin Towers) were built one behind the other identically but not in the same period, so if they are twins, it must have been a horrendously long labour. Torre dei Seretti (Secret Tower) was owned by a noble family in the village and tells their story in an intriguing fashion. The final tower is the Torre delle Quattro Porte (Tower of the Four Doors). This is unique as you can go inside it. The four arches were once doorways that gave access to the castle – look out for the two remaining medieval hinges. 🕐 10.00–12.30, 15.30–19.30 Mon–Fri, 15.30–19.30 Sat. Admission charge

CULTURE

Museo del Lavoro della Civiltà Rurale

This agricultural museum displays examples of old farming equipment and machinery used in the Tuscan area. The equipment is set in motion on the first Sunday of September only. ⓐ San Gervasio, Palaia ⓣ (0587) 484 361 ⓔ info@comune.palaia.pisa.it 🕐 Open by appointment only

Museo del Legno

The museum's displays of tools and carpentry equipment used through the ages and demonstrations of wood-working techniques used in furniture making may not sound tremendously rock'n'roll; but they leave the visitor with a sense of awe at the ingenuity and artistry possessed by the rural folk of the area. ⓐ Piazza della Mostra 4, Ponsacco ⓣ (0587) 731 102 ⓦ www.mostramobilio.it ⓛ 09.00–12.30, 15.00–19.30

TAKING A BREAK

Bar Aurora £ With a perfect location in the square near the fountain, this bar serves pasta, salted bread sandwiches and ice cream. ⓐ Vicopisano ⓣ (050) 796 298 ⓛ 09.30–19.00

Osteria di San Giuliano £ A quick lunch of seasonal produce or a full dinner with fresh pasta and game sauces is offered here, and during the summer months a wide range of just-caught fish is served. The menu changes according to what is available and in season. ⓐ Largo Shelley 20, San Giuliano Terme ⓣ (050) 815 288 ⓛ 12.30–14.30, 19.30–22.30 Mon–Sat

AFTER DARK

La Lanterna Blu £ The toothsome Tuscan pizzas here are devised by a very creative chef. There's a terrace outside and it's a short walk from Lenzi's B&B (see page 114). ⓐ Via Provinciale Francesca Nord 5, Vicopisano ⓣ (050) 798 669 ⓛ 12.30–15.00, 19.00–21.00 Tues–Sun

Taverna degli Olivi £ A cheeky little spot that serves pizza and such Tuscan specialities as *pasta al cinghiale* (pasta with wild boar sauce). There's an outdoor terrace that's glorious during the summer months. ⓐ Via della Verruca 7, Località Luchetta ⓣ (050) 799 938 ⓛ 19.00–21.00 Tues–Sun ⓘ Opens for lunch only on request, which should be made by phone

Ristorante Le Arcate ££ Situated in a magnificent villa, this was the summer residence of the Poschi family, who have wielded power and influence in these parts since medieval times. It has a beautifully frescoed dining room and serves scrumptious Tuscan food. ⓐ Via Statale Abetone, Pugnano di San Giuliano Terme ⓣ (050) 850 105 ⓛ 12.00–14.00, 19.30–00.00 ⓦ www.villaposchi.it

ACCOMMODATION

B&B Terricciola £ An absolute gem that has five apartments, a babysitting service and can easily and effectively accommodate disabled guests. There's even a lovely swimming pool. ⓐ Via Boccanera 12, Terricciola ⓣ (0587) 654 085 ⓔ g.cinzia@tin.it ⓘ Credit cards not accepted

Il Frutteto £ Attractive B&B with rooms named after fruits, to match the orchards among which this big house is situated. There are also apartments to rent. ⓐ Via Tonnaia 4, Lari ⓣ (0587) 687 078 ⓦ www.ilfrutteto.net ⓘ Extra fee for air conditioning and laundry

Lenzi's B&B £ 'We've done our best when we see you rest' is

⬥ *The relaxing outdoor terrace at Lenzi's B&B, Vicopisano*

the felicitously rhyming translation of the motto of this lovely guesthouse that offers a choice of four en suite rooms. Next door there's a ceramic workshop where you can watch the master potter making beautiful terracotta vases. ⓐ Viale Armando Diaz 83, Vicopisano ⓣ (050) 799 015 ⓦ www.lenzi.pisa.it

Villa di Corliano £££ This was the residence of Count Agostini Venerosi della Seta, an influential medieval bigwig. Restored to its natural beauty, all the rooms have antique furniture and the old cellar is now the breakfast room. There's an elegant restaurant and a romantic private garden which both add to the appeal of this magnificent hotel whose beauty it is difficult to overstate. ⓐ Strada Statale Abetone 50 Rigoli, San Giuliano Terme ⓣ (050) 818 193 ⓦ www.ussero.com

Val di Cecina

The Cecina valley, which stretches to 70 km (43 miles) southeast of Pisa, is dotted with lovely villages that you really should investigate while you're in the area.

The biggest is Volterra, a beautiful settlement that's absolutely filled with places of interest, including a cathedral (see page 118), palaces, museums, Roman baths and an Etruscan burial site. Situated in a green landscape with hills all around it, Volterra is well known for its alabaster stonework. Every July it hosts a **jazz festival** ( www.volterra-jazz.net), and from 15 October until 15 November there's a food festival every weekend.

The upper Cecina valley also has some fabulous places to explore, places that are so small that they may have only one or two features of interest; but of interest they certainly are, and taken together or singly, they captivate.

Montecatini Val di Cecina was originally an Etruscan settlement, although its heyday didn't really arrive until well into the Middle Ages. Its many medieval buildings are sandwiched together by narrow streets and alleyways and offer labyrinthine delight. The neighbouring village of Montegemoli has a castle with a Renaissance tower, while the the village of Pomarance has two impressive gateways – Porta di Casale and Porta Orciolina – that date back to the 14th century. The village of Montecastelli has its own fascinating massive medieval tower and a cemetery that accommodates an eerie Etruscan statue called *Buca delle Fate* (The Fairy Hole). The village of Castelnuovo is surrounded by woodlands and nearby Sasso Pisano also has a castle.

● *Palazzo dei Priori, Volterra*

GETTING THERE

Volterra is approximately 60 km (37 miles) southeast from Pisa
by car. Follow the SS206 road and then turn on to the SS439
road. The car parks outside of Volterra's city walls are free. The
underground car park in Piazza Martiri della Libertà and the
Parcheggio La Stazione at the station both charge a fee to park
for the day. You'll reach Montecatini Val di Cecina via the SS439
road – the impressive tower dominates the pretty Etruscan
village so you can't miss it. Trains run to Cecina (for details call
❶ (0586) 680 684); buses run to Castelnuovo, Montecastelli,
La Sassa, Pomarance and Volterra (call ❶ (0588) 673 70 for
information on all routes). For buses to Volterra, call
❶ (0588) 861 50.

SIGHTS & ATTRACTIONS

Duomo (Cathedral)

The interior of Volterra's cathedral, which was constructed between
the 13th and 15th centuries, is brimming with artistic delights,
chief of which is its pulpit, which contains some beautiful relief
work. The high point of these is the so-called 'Last Supper' section,
with its ominous nods to the fate of Judas, who almost overwhelms
the Christ figure. Just next to the altar is a fine wood carving
from 1228 called *Deposition*. Interestingly, it has been re-painted
in its original colours and these seem almost unnaturally vivid
to eyes used to seeing decorations that have faded over time.
ⓐ Piazza San Giovanni, Volterra ⓒ 08.00–19.00

THE PALAZZI OF VOLTERRA

As well as the Palazzo dei Priori (see below), Volterra boasts a number of other palaces that are not open to the public but are nonetheless well worth admiring from the outside. **Palazzo Pretorio** and the **Porcellino tower** (both ⓐ Piazza dei Priori) are fascinating. The former shows quite clearly that it is in fact several structures from different ages rather inelegantly melded into one. The Tower of the Little Pig is so-called because at its base you can see a little stone animal. **Palazzo Vescovile** (ⓐ Via Roma) was built as a grain store and has some interesting arches that have so far defied serious categorisation. **Palazzo Incontri** (ⓐ Via Roma) is now a bank but is worth admiring for its medieval and Renaissance architecture, especially the carvings on its façade.

Palazzo dei Priori

This impressive building, which was completed in 1208, has a three-storey façade and double arched windows. On the wall are the glazed terracotta coats of arms of Della Robbia (Florentine magistrates). The Council Hall has a cross vaulted ceiling and shows the fresco of The Annunciation, featuring evocative depictions of four saints, Cosmas, Damian, Giusto and Ottaviano. ⓐ Piazza dei Priori, Volterra ⓣ (0588) 872 57 ⓛ 10.30–17.30 Mon–Fri, 10.00–17.00 Sat & Sun, Mar–Nov. Admission charge

Teatro Romano & Arco Etrusco

Just outside Volterra are the ruins of a Roman theatre that dates

▲ *Part of Teatro Romano in Volterra*

back to the first century BC. The seating is still visible and this is one of the best-preserved theatres in Italy: it's impossible not to be transported back to the days when it would have been a hub of the area's cultural life. You can also see the remains of thermal baths and parts of a village. Another, much older, relic is an Etruscan Arch that bears effigies of what are thought to be gods. ❸ Just outside Volterra ⏰ 10.30–19.30. Admission charge

CULTURE

Museo Etrusco Guarnacci

Mario Guarnacci, a celebrated historian (1701–85), was also a hoarder of ancient artefacts, and his collection of over a thousand pieces (including 600 funeral urns) is on show at this superb museum, just outside Volterra. Tomb furniture and bronze works are on display, including some statues whose simple, mournful casting are terribly moving. There is also a fabulous Roman mosaic, but the star exhibit is the renowned *Ombra della Sera*, a wildly elongated nude figurine. ❸ Via Don Minzoni 15, Volterra ☎ (0588) 863 47 🌐 www.volterraonline.it ⏰ 09.00–19.00 Mar–Nov; 09.00–13.00 Dec–Feb. Admission charge

Museo delle Miniere

It's well worth taking a guided tour of this ninth-century copper mine, if only to admire the ingenuity with which its contents were extracted. ❸ Piazza Garibaldi, Montecatini Val di Cecina ☎ (0588) 310 26 🌐 www.museodelleminiere.it ⏰ Tours on the hour 15.00–18.00 Mon–Fri, 11.00–12.00, 15.00–18.00 Sat & Sun. Admission charge ❶ Advance booking required

Museo della Tortura

The Museum of Torture, which sits innocently just beyond Volterra, is not for wimps! Hundreds of not-very-subtle devices of persuasion from the Inquisition onwards are on display and are gruesomely compelling. Racks and masks with spikes on the inside are the least of it. These days, the museum works with Amnesty International to try to prevent the torture that still goes on around the world. ⓐ Piazza XX Settembre 3, Volterra ⓣ (0588) 805 01 ⓦ www.museodellatortura.com ⓛ 10.00–19.00. Admission charge

🔺 *This area of Tuscany is famous for its alabaster stone works*

RETAIL THERAPY

Alabaster Store Alabaster is big around these parts, having been mined here for centuries until just after World War II. This shop has a vast selection of gifts, and, if you're looking for a bespoke item, its owners can put you in touch with the dwindling number of craftspeople who use this porous form of chalk as a sculptural medium. ⓐ Piazza dei Priori 5, Volterra ⓣ (0588) 875 90 ⓦ www.artierialabastro.it ⓛ 10.00–18.00

Montagnani Spartaco Bronze Statues The name says it all, and there's a large selection of bronze objects, statues, jewellery and trinkets to browse over. Great for gifts. ⓐ Via Porta all'Arco 6, Volterra ⓣ (0588) 861 84 ⓛ 10.00–17.30 Mon–Sat

TAKING A BREAK

Bar Priori £ Cosy local meeting place that serves sandwiches, snacks, drinks and ice cream. ⓐ Piazza dei Priori 2, Volterra ⓣ (0588) 862 10 ⓛ 08.00–19.30

Pasticceria Bracaloni £ A good selection of cakes, biscuits and bread, which you can enjoy on the spot or snaffle away for a picnic. ⓐ Via Gramsci 36, Volterra ⓣ (0588) 879 32 ⓛ 08.00–18.00

AFTER DARK

Web & Wine £ Internet café and Tuscan fare restaurant with a remarkable crystal floor area that allows visitors to peek at the

progress of excavations from the one-time Etruscan settlement upon which this venue was built. ⓐ Via Porta all'Arco, Volterra ⓘ (0588) 815 31 ⓦ www.webandwine.com ⓛ 09.00–23.30

Da Badò ££ Family-run trattoria with a limited menu of local classics topped off with some delicious desserts. ⓐ Borgo San Lazzero 9, Volterra ⓘ (0588) 864 77 ⓛ 19.00–22.00 Thur–Tues

Il Margone ££ A charming, brightly decorated restaurant with lovely bay windows. Specialises in pizza and spaghetti dishes. ⓐ Località Miniere 3, Montecatini Val di Cecina ⓘ (0588) 303 96 ⓛ 18.00–00.00 summer only (winter by prior arrangment)

Ristorante Enoteca Del Duca £££ Award-winning restaurant in a medieval building with an impressive wine list and a Tuscan menu that changes to reflect what's in season. Enjoying a meal late in the evening under canopies on the terrace is an unforgettable experience. ⓐ Via di Castello 2, Volterra ⓘ (0588) 815 10 ⓛ 12.00–00.00 Wed–Sun ⓦ www.enoteca-delduca-ristorante.it

ACCOMMODATION

Agrihotel Il Palagetto ££ Great-value 3-star hotel in a building that goes back to Roman times. Some rooms have four-poster beds and hydro massage tubs. ⓐ Location Cozzano, Volterra ⓘ (0588) 422 21 ⓦ www.ilpalagetto.com

Agriturismo Centopino ££ Rustic-style farmhouse with a swimming pool. There are rooms to let and internet access available.

⬥ *Web & Wine with its amazing crystal floor*

Via Centopino, Montecastelli Pisano (0588) 204 28
www.agriturismocentopino.it

Agriturismo Podernuovo ££ Three large holiday flats to let on a friendly family farm. On a clear day you can see the island of Corsica. Località Podernuovo di Querceto, Montecatini Val di Cecina (0588) 374 56 www.volterra-toscana.net/provincia

Agriturismo Sancarlo ££ An in-the-middle-of-nowhere treat. You won't feel abandoned as there's a customer service desk where you can find out where to go and what to see. The owners make their own olive oil and wine, which is on sale to guests. Holiday flats are available to rent all year round. Località San Carlo, Pomarance (0588) 653 49 www.sancarloagriturismo.it

Hotel San Lino ££ This ultra-modern 4-star hotel has standard or superior rooms that used to be nuns' sleeping quarters. There's a restaurant and swimming pool and two rooms that are accessible for disabled guests. Via San Lino 26, Volterra (0588) 852 50 www.hotelsanlino.com

● *Pisa Centrale train station is very close to the city centre*

Directory

GETTING THERE
By air
Galileo Galilei airport (see page 48) has one terminal serving twenty air carriers, and flights arrive from 57 destinations around the world every day. The main carriers who fly to and from the UK are:

British Airways Ⓦ www.britishairways.com
easyJet Ⓦ www.easyjet.com
Ryanair Ⓦ www.ryanair.com
SkyEurope Ⓦ www.skyeurope.com
Transavia Ⓦ www.transavia.com

Many people are aware that air travel emits CO_2, which contributes to climate change. You may be interested in the

🔺 *Galileo Galilei International Airport*

possibility of lessening the environmental impact of your flight through **Climate Care** (Ⓦ www.climatecare.org), which offsets your CO_2 by funding environmental projects around the world.

By rail

From Britain, Eurostar travels from St Pancras International in London to Gard du Nord in Paris, where you can change for Nice and then Genoa. Pisa is on the Rome–Genoa train line. All in all, travelling from the UK to Pisa will take the best part of a tiring day, but, if you have the time, offers the wonderful experience of watching the Tuscan countryside unfold.

If you are travelling within Italy, Trenitalia offers some great deals on multi-day train passes. Wherever you are travelling from, Rail Europe is a great source of information and advice.

Eurostar ⓘ 0875 186 186 Ⓦ www.eurostar.com

Rail Europe Ⓦ www.raileurope.co.uk

Trenitalia (national trains) ⓘ 892021 (from Italy)/ 0039 06 6847 5475 (from abroad) Ⓦ www.trenitalia.com

The monthly *Thomas Cook European Rail Timetable* has up-to-date schedules for European international and national train services.

Thomas Cook European Rail Timetable ⓘ (UK) 01733 416477, (USA) 1 800 322 3834 Ⓦ www.thomascookpublishing.com

By road

If you plan to drive to Italy, it will be necessary to follow the rules of the country's roads. Speed limits are: for motorways, 130 kmh (80 miles per hour); for main roads, 110 kmh (68 miles per hour); for roads outside built-up areas, 90 kmh (55 miles per hour); for roads in built-up areas, 50 kmh (31 miles per hour). In terms of insurance, you will need to arrange a *carta verde* (green card) for the duration of your stay, for details of which you should contact your embassy or travel agent. Seat belts are compulsory for everybody, and using a hand-held phone while driving is illegal. The legal limit for blood alcohol while driving is 0.08 per cent (0.25mg/l), and Italian traffic police can and do carry out random testing. It is safest and wisest not to have drunk any alcohol at all if you plan to be behind the wheel.

Most Italian motorways operate a toll system, and you can pay with any major credit card. Do note that you will not be able to drive in the historic centre of Pisa. In the case of car breakdown call **Automobile Club D'Italia** (❶ 803 116) or **Europ Assistance Vai** (❶ 803 803). To check traffic flow and motorway access call ❶ 840 042121.

ENTRY FORMALITIES

British citizens will need a valid passport in order to enter Italy. All other European Union (EU) citizens can enter the country by producing either a valid passport or a national identity card from their own country. All EU citizens may stay in the country for as long as they wish. Citizens of the United States, Canada, Australia and New Zealand need a valid passport, but are limited to stays of three months at a time; if you wish to stay longer, leave the country briefly then go back for another three-month period. Non-EU citizens have a limit on customs alcohol and cigarettes: 400 cigarettes, 200 cigars or 500 grams of tobacco; 1 litre of spirits or 2 litres of wine; 20 grams of perfume; €10,640 in cash.

MONEY

Italy's official currency is the euro (€). There are seven banknotes: €5, €10, €20, €50, €100, €200, €500. Coin denominations are: €1, €2 and 1, 2, 5, 10, 20, 50 cents. Most banks have a 24-hour cashpoint or ATM located outside, which accepts credit cards and debit cards with Cirrus and Maestro symbols. Banks are generally open 08.20–13.20 and 14.30–16.00 from Monday to Friday. They are closed on public holidays and work shorter hours on the day before a bank holiday. Traveller's cheques can be exchanged in banks, hotels or bureaux de change for a small commission. You can also exchange money at post offices, which have a fixed commission per transaction.

HEALTH, SAFETY & CRIME

There are no particular health precautions for visiting Italy. Tap water is safe to drink but generally is used for cooking and cleaning: bottled water is favoured for drinking. Beware of the sign acqua non potabile in bathrooms and toilets, which means that the water isn't safe to drink.

Be sure to take sun cream for the summer months and always walk around with a small bottle of water to keep yourself hydrated. Wear a hat and sunglasses when sightseeing and always use after-sun to rehydrate your skin. Mosquitoes are a problem in Tuscany, as in most of Italy, particularly in the summer, but all pharmacies will be well equipped with insect repellents.

EU citizens are entitled to the same health care as Italians but you must have your **European Health Insurance Card** (EHIC, ⓣ 0845 606 2030 ⓦ www.ehic.org.uk) with you in order to get prescriptions or to see a doctor. The E111 form is no longer valid.

Both EU and non-EU citizens are advised to take out insurance, both for medical and other emergencies.

There is very little crime in Pisa. As long as you observe the basic rules of safety that you would in any town or city, you'd be very unlucky to be a victim of crime. In terms of street hassle, the city is mercifully free of stereotypical Italian machismo. If you do experience crime, contact the police (see page 138).

OPENING HOURS

The majority of shops, services, museums and attractions open at 09.00 and close at 19.30, with lunch breaks of two to three hours. Many chain stores, large department stores and services such as dentists, estate agents, private clinics and car hire don't close for lunch. Post offices usually open only in the morning, from 09.00 to 12.00, except the main branch in the city centre which opens in the afternoon until 19.30. Government buildings have their own opening hours and days of opening. All shops and places of interest have a day of closing which is normally shown on the door as you enter. Monday is generally a bad day for shopping with most shops choosing to close in the morning. Quite a few restaurants are closed on Monday night.

TOILETS

Public toilets can be found at the train station, the airport, the parking areas and near Ponte di Mezzo under the Logge dei Banchi in Via dei Banchi. There are no baby-changing facilities in Pisa. Bars, cafés and shops may have toilets, and if you need to make use of them, it's polite to ask owners or staff before you do. The standard of tidiness and hygiene of the particular establishment will be a good gauge of the likely condition of its toilets.

CHILDREN

Pisa is a good city for families. It's not the place to come if you want theme park pizzazz, but the area's natural beauty will delight – and should have a calming effect – on little ones. It is an ideal environment in which to foster an interest in antiquity in slightly older children. The city's flat streets, large squares, open spaces and the river wall make it generally a safe place to walk around. What is missing, not just in Pisa but in the whole of Italy, are baby-changing rooms and feeding facilities. Most Italian parents with young babies go back to their cars for nappy changing and breastfeeding. Pharmacies in Pisa sell all types of baby equipment, but it's best to bring any medications and items that you normally use with you. Pharmacies in Pisa don't always have English-speaking staff and the medications used here may have different names. Baby food will also have a different taste.

Restaurants and bars accept children warmly, and some may supply high chairs and will have no problems in heating milk or providing a children's dish of food if you ask nicely. 3- or 4-star hotels may offer babysitting services and put cots in the room on request.

Do note that children under the age of eight are not allowed to climb the Leaning Tower for security reasons.

COMMUNICATION
Internet

To use the internet, you can go to one of the many internet

cafés around the city. A lot of hotels also have internet access.
Three reliable, centrally located internet cafés are:

Internet Planet ⓐ Piazza Cavallotti 3 ⓣ (050) 830 702
ⓦ www.internetplanet.it ⓛ 10.00–21.00

Internet Point Koinè ⓐ Via dei Mille 3 ⓣ (050) 830 701
ⓦ www.koinepisa.it ⓛ 10.00–20.00

Internet Surf ⓐ Via Carducci 5 ⓣ (050) 830 800
ⓦ www.internetsurf.it ⓛ 10.00–00.00

Phone

You can buy a *scheda telefonica* (phonecard) from *tabacchi*
(tobacconist shops), and this will allow you to use one of the ever-
decreasing public phones. Most people now use mobile phones.
Mobile numbers in Italy start with the number 3, for example,
333, 347, 339 and 340, and you should contact your supplier to

TELEPHONING ITALY

The international country code for Italy is +39, preceded by
the international code (oo from UK and New Zealand, o11 from
the USA, oo11 from Australia). The city code for Pisa is o5o.

TELEPHONING ABROAD

Dial oo, the international access code, followed by your
country code and then the area code minus the initial zero
followed by the number itself. Some of the major country
codes are: UK: 44; Ireland: 353; France: 33; Germany: 49; USA: 1;
Canada: 1; Australia: 61; New Zealand: 64; South Africa: 27

◯ *You can find Italian red mail boxes on street walls*

arrange roaming. In Italy 800 numbers are freephone information numbers. To call directory enquiries, dial ☎ 1240.

Post

The main post office is in Piazza Vittorio Emanuele. Stamps are called *francobolli* and both letters and postcards currently cost 65 cents to send to Europe. The post boxes are red and have two slots. Use the slot marked *altre destinazioni* when sending mail abroad. For maximum reliability when sending letters, most people use *Posta Prioritaria*, which is a little more expensive, needs a special sticker and requires use of a separate box, which is either marked *Posta Prioritaria* or coloured blue. Stamps can be bought either at the post office or in tobacconist shops.

ELECTRICITY

Electricity runs on 220V AC. Plugs are two-pin Continental-style, so you'll need an adapter for any electrical products you bring with you from the UK. Buying an adapter to use in Italy may be difficult so it's best to bring one with you.

TRAVELLERS WITH DISABILITIES

Pisa is generally wheelchair-friendly, with flat pavements and not many steps to go in and out of buildings and shops. The shopping districts and the Campo dei Miracoli are easily accessible by wheelchair, and some hotels and restaurants have facilities for disabled guests. Details on disabled facilities in Italy can be found on the **Italian Ministry of Health**'s website (Ⓦ www.sanita.it), and another useful website is Ⓦ www.disabili.com. **Accessible Italy** (Ⓣ (0549) 941 111 Ⓦ www.accessibleitaly.com) is an English organisation that offers disabled travellers help and advice, search for transport facilities, accommodation booking and they do mini-van rides with an English speaking driver.

TOURIST INFORMATION

Agenzia per il Turismo Pisa (Pisa Tourist Board) ⓐ Via Matteucci Galleria Gerace 14 Ⓣ (050) 929 777 Ⓦ www.pisaturismo.it Ⓛ 09.00–13.00 Mon, Wed & Fri, 09.00–13.00, 15.00–17.00 Tues & Thur, 09.00–13.00 Sat
There are also branches at:
APT Pisa ⓐ Piazza Vittorio Emanuele II 16 Ⓣ (050) 422 91 Ⓛ 09.00–19.00 Mon–Fri
APT Pisa Airport ⓐ Piazzale Corradino D'Ascanio Ⓣ (050) 502 518 Ⓛ 11.00–23.00

If you are heading out of town, try the following sources of tourist information:

Consorzio Turistico Volterra Val di Cecina Valdera ⓐ Piazza dei Priori 20, Volterra ⓣ (0588) 872 57 ⓦ www.volterratur.it ⓛ 10.00–13.00, 14.00–18.00

Lari ⓐ Piazza delle Mura 2 ⓣ (0587) 684 125 ⓦ www.prolocolari.it ⓛ 10.00–17.00 Mon–Sat

Proloco-San Giuliano Terme ⓐ Via Roma 29 ⓣ (050) 815 064 ⓦ www.comune.sangiulianoterme.pisa.it ⓛ 10.00–18.00 Mon–Sat

Vicopisano Turismo ⓐ Via Lante 1A ⓣ (050) 796276 ⓦ www.viconet.it

Another useful resource is the **English Yellow Pages** for Italy, which gives reference to English speaking shops and services in some of Italy's most visited towns. See ⓦ www.englishyellowpages.it

BACKGROUND READING

Discovering Wine Country Tuscany by Monty Waldin and Tony McTerran. A most instructive wine trail through the many villages of Tuscany.

The Knights Templar: History and Myths of the Legendary Military Order by Sean Marin. Weird sect and precursors to the Masons? Superb fighting force of mavericks and maniacs? This fascinating read gives much insight into the Christian fundamentalist SAS of the Middle Ages.

Emergencies

The following are emergency free-call numbers:

Ambulance (Ambulanza) ⓘ 118
Carabinieri ⓘ 112
Police (Polizia Municipale) ⓘ 113 or (050) 910 811
Fire (Vigili dei Fuoco) ⓘ 115

MEDICAL SERVICES

Though not massively endowed with medical services, Pisa has all the facilities any visitor is likely to require. **Hospital Santa Chiara** (ⓔ Via Roma 67 ⓘ (050) 992 111) is perfectly well equipped to take care of any emergencies and is also the place to call if you need to speak to a doctor for advice on minor ailments or if you need to be put in touch with a dentist. Another great source of advice is **Farmacia Comunale** (ⓔ Via Niccolini 6 ⓘ (050) 560 258), a 24-hour pharmacy for emergency prescriptions or medication of any kind.

POLICE

If you are the victim of crime, you need to call the *Carabinieri* (police) or go to the nearest *Questura* (police station). The main police station is on Via Mario Lalli 1 (ⓘ 050 583 511). You will need to explain what has happened and you will be asked to sign a statement. If you are arrested, the best option is to call the British Consulate in Florence, whose staff can give procedural (but not legal) advice. In Italy you can be held for three years without trial.

EMERGENCY PHRASES

Help!
Aiuto!
Ahyootaw!

Fire!
Al fuoco!
Ahl fooawcaw!

Stop!
Ferma!
Fairmah!

Call an ambulance/a doctor/the police/the fire service!
Chiamate un'ambulanza/un medico/la polizia/i pompieri!
Kyahmahteh oon ahmboolahntsa/oon mehdeecaw/
la pawleetsya/ee pompee-ehree!

Lost or stolen credit cards
American Express ☎ 06 7 22 82
Diners Club ☎ 800 86 40 64
MasterCard ☎ 800 87 08 66
Visa ☎ 800 87 72 32

EMBASSIES & CONSULATES
All of the main embassies and consulates are in Florence or Rome:
Australian Embassy @ Via Antonio Bosio 5, Rome ☎ (06) 852 721
🌐 www.italy.embassy.gov.au
British Consulate @ Lungarno Corsini 2, Florence ☎ (055) 284 133
🕐 08.00–12.00, 13.00–16.00 Mon–Fri 🌐 www.britain.it
US Consulate General @ Lungarno Vespucci 38, Florence
☎ (055) 266 951

Send your thoughts to
books@thomascook.com

- Found a great bar, club, shop or must-see sight that we don't feature?

- Like to tip us off about any information that needs a little updating?

- Want to tell us what you love about this handy little guidebook and more importantly how we can make it even handier?

Then here's your chance to tell all! Send us ideas, discoveries and recommendations today and then look out for your valuable input in the next edition of this title.

Email the above address (stating the title) or write to: CitySpots Series Editor, Thomas Cook Publishing, PO Box 227, Coningsby Road, Peterborough PE3 8SB, UK.

SPOTTED YOUR NEXT CITY BREAK?

...then these lightweight CitySpots pocket guides will have you in the know in no time, wherever you're heading.

Covering over 90 cities worldwide, they're packed with detail on the most important urban attractions from shopping and sights to non-stop nightlife; knocking spots off chunkier, clunkier versions.

Aarhus
Amsterdam
Antwerp
Athens
Bangkok
Barcelona
Belfast
Belgrade
Berlin
Biarritz
Bilbao
Bologna
Bordeaux
Bratislava
Bruges
Brussels
Bucharest
Budapest
Cairo
Cape Town
Cardiff
Cologne
Copenhagen
Cork
Dubai
Dublin
Dubrovnik
Düsseldorf
Edinburgh
Fez
Florence
Frankfurt

Gdansk
Geneva
Genoa
Glasgow
Gothenburg
Granada
Hamburg
Hanover
Helsinki
Hong Kong
Istanbul
Kiev
Krakow
Kuala Lumpur
Leipzig
Lille
Lisbon
Liverpool
Ljubljana
London
Los Angeles
Lyon
Madrid
Marrakech
Marseilles
Milan
Monte Carlo
Moscow
Munich
Naples
New York City
Nice

Oslo
Palermo
Palma
Paris
Pisa
Prague
Porto
Reykjavik
Riga
Rome
Rotterdam
Salzburg
Sarajevo
Seville
Singapore
Sofia
Stockholm
Strasbourg
St Petersburg
Tallinn
Tirana
Tokyo
Toulouse
Turin
Valencia
Venice
Verona
Vienna
Vilnius
Warsaw
Zagreb
Zurich

Available from all good bookshops, your local Thomas Cook travel store or browse and buy online at www.thomascookpublishing.com

Thomas Cook Publishing

Editorial/project management: Lisa Plumridge
Copy editor: Paul Hines
Layout/DTP: Alison Rayner
Picture editor: Sonia Marotta
Proofreader: Judy Johnson

The publishers would like to thank the following individuals
and organisations for supplying their copyright photographs for
this book: Archivio Consorzio Turistico Volterra, pages 103 & 117;
Paolo Bassetti, page 111; Scott Brenner, page 25; cidibee, page 11;
Jonatha Borzicchi/Dreamstime.com, pages 14–5; Lenzi's B&B,
page 115; Philip Lange/Dreamstime.com, page 45; Sonia Marotta,
pages 7, 21, 23, 29, 47, 49, 69 & 135; Rosy Mussari, pages 1, 9, 17, 19, 22,
26, 38, 40–1, 43, 57, 59, 65, 67, 75, 80, 86, 91, 95, 127 & 128; Riccardo
Remorini/Pappafico, page 73; Residence Club Cosmopolitan Golf,
page 34; Linda Z Ryan/BigStockPhoto.com, page 122; Ralph Unden,
page 105; Web&Wine, page 125; James Whisker, page 120.